COVID-19 AND ENERGY SECTOR DEVELOPMENT IN ASIA AND THE PACIFIC

GUIDANCE NOTE

JUNE 2021

ASIAN DEVELOPMENT BANK

ADB

© 2021 Asian Development Bank
6 ADB Avenue, Mandaluyong City, 1550 Metro Manila, Philippines
Tel +63 2 8632 4444; Fax +63 2 8636 2444
www.adb.org

Some rights reserved. Published in 2021.

ISBN 978-92-9262-907-6 (print); 978-92-9262-908-3 (electronic); 978-92-9262-909-0 (ebook)
Publication Stock No. TIM210204
DOI: http://dx.doi.org/10.22617/TIM210204

The views expressed in this publication are those of the authors and do not necessarily reflect the views and policies of the Asian Development Bank (ADB) or its Board of Governors or the governments they represent.

ADB does not guarantee the accuracy of the data included in this publication and accepts no responsibility for any consequence of their use. The mention of specific companies or products of manufacturers does not imply that they are endorsed or recommended by ADB in preference to others of a similar nature that are not mentioned.

By making any designation of or reference to a particular territory or geographic area, or by using the term "country" in this document, ADB does not intend to make any judgments as to the legal or other status of any territory or area.

Please contact pubsmarketing@adb.org if you have questions or comments with respect to content, or if you wish to obtain copyright permission for your intended use that does not fall within these terms, or for permission to use the ADB logo.

Corrigenda to ADB publications may be found at http://www.adb.org/publications/corrigenda.

Notes:
In this publication, "$" refers to United States dollars.
ADB recognizes "China" as the People's Republic of China.

On the cover: The coronavirus disease (COVID-19) pandemic has underscored the importance of reliable, affordable, and uninterrupted energy supply. Energy systems operated reliably during the pandemic but were placed under increased technical and economic stress (photos by Al Benavente, M.A. Pushpa Kumara, Nozim Kalandarov, Gerhard Joren, Eric Sales/ADB).

Cover design by Nonie Villanueva.

Contents

Tables and Figures

Abbreviations

ADB	Asian Development Bank
COVID-19	coronavirus disease
DMC	developing member country
GHG	greenhouse gas
GW	gigawatt
IEA	International Energy Agency
IRENA	International Renewable Energy Agency
LNG	liquified natural gas
NO$_2$	nitrogen dioxide
O&M	operation and maintenance
PLN	Perusahaan Listrik Negara (Indonesia)
PM2.5	particulate matter
PRC	People's Republic of China
PV	photovoltaic
SDG	Sustainable Development Goal

Executive Summary

While the coronavirus disease (COVID-19) has resulted in a severe global health and economic crisis, it also presents an opportunity for a green, sustainable, and resilient recovery. The International Energy Agency (IEA) estimates that the pandemic will result in at least a 5% decrease in global energy demand and a 7% decrease in global energy-related greenhouse gas (GHG) emissions in 2020, but at the cost of severe economic effects. The recovery phase, in which stimulus funding will be needed, can be oriented to support the transition to a low-carbon energy system, while at the same time support economic recovery through job creation and provision of required fundamental quality energy infrastructure.

The Asian Development Bank (ADB) is supporting its developing member countries (DMCs) as they struggle to manage primarily the health crisis, and then will continue to support DMCs during the recovery phase to address economic effects brought about by reduced international travel and trade, along with contractions of domestic economies. In this context, ADB will support continued development progress, reinforcing the need for modern energy systems to meet United Nations Sustainable Development Goals (SDGs) by focusing support on technologies and sector policies aligned with the reduction of air pollution and support for low-carbon transition as committed under the Paris Agreement.

Energy supply and system operation in Asia and the Pacific has been able to meet demand reliably during the pandemic despite concerns over personnel shortages and travel restrictions that put limitations on operations and maintenance. This, for example, has enabled hospitals to provide health care services, and also allowed employees to work from home to help businesses continue operations and allow daily life to continue, in general. For the energy sector, the main effects have included (i) declining commodity prices for fossil fuels (including oil, natural gas, and coal) due to decreased demand globally; (ii) a decline in overall power demand, but with increased demand in the residential sector; and (iii) limitations in personnel mobility that has slowed project development and implementation of new energy infrastructure.

For energy suppliers, the economic effects have been severe and can be long-lasting. Reductions in energy demand due to COVID-19 lockdowns have reduced revenue, but operational costs have not decreased. For end users, reduced prices of some energy sources have resulted in savings (such as reduced diesel prices for fossil fuel-based power production). But retail prices for power have not decreased for ordinary consumers, and therefore increased residential power use (due to the lockdowns) has resulted in increased personal energy expenses that are a burden for those in lower socioeconomic groups.

Power utilities have been one of the most severely affected, many of whom were not in strong financial shape before the pandemic. These utilities have experienced the combination of decreased revenues as demand declined and then reduced payment from end-consumers who are less able to pay due to the effects of the pandemic. Many governments have provided financial support to both end users and energy utilities to mitigate these issues, and this could affect the ability to finance longer-term investments.

As activity shifts from the initial response to economic recovery, DMCs face both a tremendous challenge and opportunity. Ongoing development needs, commitments under the Paris Agreement, and aiming to achieve SDGs provide a clear direction for economic recovery actions. Focus on the energy sector can ensure a reliable supply of sustainable energy to support economic activity and essential services, while investments and job creation can provide economic stimulus directly. Investment in the energy sector can be part of a holistic approach to a low-carbon and resilient recovery, and can be framed as "Recovery through Rejuvenation and Resilience" that rests on the following interrelated four pillars:

(i) enhancing sustainable energy services,
(ii) improving energy sector resilience and security,
(iii) accelerating energy access to the poor and vulnerable, and
(iv) using advanced technology and cross-sector interventions.

Enhancing sustainable energy services is an ongoing development imperative, but has become clearer during the pandemic. Most DMCs experience some level of energy inadequacy, from high levels of unmet demand to high annual outage levels, as well as regional disparities within countries. Renewable energy deployments—especially for solar and wind—can now produce power that is lower in cost than coal and gas in many countries, providing the economic motivation to deploy these technologies to harvest indigenous renewable resources. Alongside this, strong and robust electricity grids will also be needed, as well as energy efficiency to reduce growing energy demand, while countries develop. ADB is well-placed to support these investments along with strengthening governance, policy, and planning that may otherwise prove to be a weak link in the transition to lower-carbon energy systems. Aligning these investments with COVID-19 recovery stimulus can leverage development progress, while meeting climate change goals and ensuring that energy infrastructure is in place to meet cold chain requirements for COVID-19 vaccine delivery.

Improving energy sector resilience and security has been clearly identified as a need during the COVID-19 pandemic. Although the energy system has operated well so far, concerns over reliance on international access to skills and capabilities, technologies, and fuel resources mean that energy systems have been put at risk. Renewable energy technologies, when deployed and maintained with local staffing and supported by local manufacturing, improves the resilience of energy generation using indigenous energy resources. While COVID-19 has reduced the cost of imported fossil fuels, the next shock or crisis could result in limited access or spikes in global fossil fuel prices (as seen in the past), and therefore reduction in the use of imported fuels increases resilience against possible (or probable) future events.

Looking at broader and long-term resilience and security beyond the current focus, physical climate risks have not disappeared. Energy sector investments need to consider potential physical effects on infrastructure due to climate change. Investments must also ensure that infrastructure aligns with current and future climate policy, and is not stranded, resulting in wasted efforts and resources. As advanced information and communication technology is integrated into energy system, provisions for cybersecurity must also be in place. The inclusion of a holistic view of security and resilience can ensure that energy systems remain stable and reliable enablers of economic development.

Accelerating energy access to the poor and vulnerable groups has been identified as an urgent response to the pandemic. As a result of the economic effects from COVID-19, the IEA estimates that at least 110 million people, mostly in developing Africa and Asia, could lose their ability to pay for basic electricity services. During recovery, stimulus money for pro-poor and pro-vulnerable tariff structures and energy infrastructure can be prioritized to support basic services and productive use of energy. Interventions that focus on small businesses, education, and health care will be essential to support populations that have been cut off from overseas-based work opportunities due to COVID-19, ensuring that the next generation does not fall behind in education and strengthening the health care system to address current pandemic-related and future health needs. Accelerating efforts could also focus on existing gaps such as programs that support clean cooking, and women-headed households or women-led micro, small, and medium-sized enterprises, taking into account that the lower income of women has not been adequately addressed in the past.

Using advanced technology and cross-sector interventions is essential to link the three abovementioned priorities. Along with the rapid growth of solar, wind, and energy efficiency technologies, there is also a need to scale up hydrogen and carbon capture, utilization and storage, and new momentum behind nuclear power. Remote management and payment systems can enable access to energy in last-mile applications essential for cold chain infrastructure needed for vaccine deployment. Automated metering infrastructure can reduce physical contact to help prevent the spread of COVID-19, while reducing commercial losses that can be damaging for utilities. Battery storage systems can increase the efficiency of system operation and support renewable integration. Cross-sector interventions can include clean and modern waste-to-energy systems that can safely address increased medical waste during COVID-19 response, while providing needed energy supply. Providing energy to schools and health clinics as anchor loads to mini-grids, which can be then extended to communities and small businesses, are practical cross-sector interventions. These are just a few examples that can be deployed to support DMCs in meeting the first three priorities as their economies recover from the pandemic.

ADB's existing energy sector investments align well with the needs of DMCs to recover from the effects of the pandemic. From a macro level, ADB's energy sector operations will continue to focus on urgent needs as a result of the pandemic, deliver its existing pipeline of investments, and adjust existing projects to address any changes caused by COVID-19 within their respective DMCs. In this context, energy projects will be developed and implemented to consider the effects of COVID-19 and make adjustments as needed, but there is still a strong and compelling need for significant energy investments in DMCs that are aligned with the Paris Agreement, SDGs, and ADB's Strategy 2030.

There is an opportunity to accelerate efforts in the energy sector and stakeholders must work together in order to ensure that the energy needs are met to support broader societal recovery from the pandemic together with low-carbon development. The focus of response and recovery highlighted above offers a broad range of energy sector considerations that requires action, providing opportunity for ADB's energy investments to align across all sectors in support of a green recovery to meet development objectives. Cross-sector collaboration will provide ADB the opportunity to address development issues and deliver services in a truly sustainable manner in DMCs.

Solar panels gathering sun power and turbines harvesting wind power at the Burgos Wind and Solar Farm in Burgos, Ilocos Norte in the Philippines (photo by Al Benavente/Asian Development Bank).

1 Introduction

Energy supply and system operations around the globe have been able to meet demand reliably during the pandemic, despite concerns over personnel shortages throughout lockdowns and travel restrictions that put limitations on operation and maintenance (O&M). The main effects in the energy sector have included decreasing commodity prices for fossil energy (including oil, natural gas, and coal) as a result of decreased final energy demand and decrease in overall power demand, but with increased demand in the residential sector and limitations on personnel mobility which slowed down project development and implementation.[1] While the entire global energy system has been affected, the way each country has been affected varies substantially.

The coronavirus disease (COVID-19) has affected countries as a whole, but the abovementioned effects have been more acutely felt in urban centers. While commercial, public, and social services were either halted or partially restricted during lockdown, there was still a need for Required Core Urban Service Standards.[2] These service standards are broadly crosscutting and while energy is directly needed in both heating and cooling and electricity, energy remains essential in delivering all core urban services.

---

[1] Power system balance of supply and demand can be challenging during both periods of increased and decreased demand, especially when high shares of variable renewables are prioritized for dispatch during low-demand periods, increasing the share of non-dispatchable variable generation.

[2] ADB. 2020. *COVID-19 and Livable Cities in Asia and the Pacific: Guidance Note*. Manila.

During quarantine and lockdown, the measures that were put in place to prevent the spread of COVID-19 resulted in a significant reduction in pollutants due to less mobility and decreased electricity demand and industrial production (which are primarily dependent on fossil fuels). While this is a positive development in terms of air quality due to the reduction in greenhouse gases (GHGs), making these reductions permanent requires structural changes—in particular, building upon or creating policies that focus on measuring and managing urban air quality and indoor air quality to encourage energy efficiency and clean energy use.

In Metro Manila, Philippines, for example, during the first 30 days of enhanced community quarantine, fine particulate matter (PM2.5) levels were at the lowest on record. Nitrogen dioxide (NO2) levels were over 50% lower compared to 2019. While this was likely due to reduced transportation activity, large reductions in fossil fuel-based power production was also likely to have contributed to the decline in air pollution levels. When the country moved to enhanced general community quarantine, which was less restrictive, the levels of both PM2.5 and NO2 rebounded to levels seen just before the enhanced community quarantine.[3] This rebound was also seen in Delhi, India where NO2 levels dropped by over 40% during the country's COVID-19 lockdown, but had nearly rebounded to pre-COVID-19 levels by mid-August.[4]

In both the Peoples' Republic of China (PRC)[5] and in Europe,[6] satellite data have demonstrated a significant reduction of NO2 in urban centers during the time when major limitations were placed on the movement of populations and industries were shut down to stem the spread of the virus. The initial data demonstrated that while the PRC slowly reduced restrictions and brought its economy back to life, NO2 emissions increased.

While the response to dealing with the virus and the economic implications of such drastic measures is not the actual solution to addressing pollution, it does offer a vision of what clear skies look like, and the value of fresh air. Beyond these qualitative observations, it provides increased data on the sources and effects of the pollution that can be used to inform the interventions that may be used to clean the air and mitigate climate change, while at the same time providing jobs and bolstering economic activity. Annual emissions in 2020 are projected to be lower than 2019 by a significant amount, but this is not necessarily a structural change. After the 2007–2008 Great Financial Crisis, emissions rebounded to a level higher than before the crisis.

For suppliers of both primary and secondary energy, this has reduced revenue, while for many, the costs of operation have not diminished to the same degree, creating a negative financial impact. For end users, reduced prices of some energy sources have resulted in savings (such as reduced diesel prices for fossil fuel-based power production). However, unit retail prices for power have not decreased, and therefore increased residential use has resulted in increased costs that have been a burden for lower socioeconomic populations. Power utilities, many of whom were not in strong financial shape before the pandemic, have felt a major impact due to decreased demand (resulting in decreased revenue), while remaining fixed and variable costs have been combined with customers who are unable to pay due to broader economic effects of the pandemic. Such financial stressors can result in reduced O&M spending as well as decreased investment in new infrastructure, leading to lower levels of service or lack of progress to improving energy services. This may also limit countries' efforts to address energy-related emission as part of their Nationally Determined Contributions to the Paris Agreement.

---

3   Centre for Research on Energy and Clean Air. 2020. Special Report: Managing Air Quality Beyond COVID-19.
4   *The Economist*. 2020. Air Pollution is Returning to Pre-COVID Levels. 5 September.
5   The European Space Agency. 2020. COVID-19: Nitrogen Dioxide Over China. 19 March.
6   The European Space Agency. 2020. Coronavirus Lockdown Leading to Drop in Pollution Across Europe. 27 March.

The financial effects across economies caused by the COVID-19 pandemic have been significant and continue to grow for many countries. The response to these effects will require economic stimulus to rebuild and revitalize economies. Government responses to the health impacts of COVID-19 indicate a clear willingness to provide funding at scale to counter immediate public health effects. Reducing conventional pollutants (especially PM2.5, which is linked to higher risk of susceptibility to COVID-19, and NO2, which is an indicator of local air pollution and GHGs) is also attracting increased attention for investment that has not historically been forthcoming for carbon mitigation pathways envisioned under the Paris Agreement.

Orienting stimulus to support sustainable energy systems will support economic recovery from the pandemic. The former UN Secretary-General Ban Ki-moon is quoted as saying, "Energy is the golden thread that connects economic growth, increased social equity, and an environment that allows the world to thrive." Developing member countries (DMCs) of the Asian Development Bank (ADB) will increase their energy use as they develop economically. On this basis, it is expected that a share of stimulus offered in response to the economic effects of COVID-19 will flow into the energy sector. As countries consider the use of stimulus for economic rebuilding, it will be essential to make the most of these resources and may create an opportunity to address structural energy sector problems, both from a technical and policy perspective (e.g., inefficient generation, sub-cost recovery tariff structures, fossil fuel subsidies, ineffective or absent regulators, fossil fuel investments leading to future stranded asset risk in a low-carbon society).

Many low-carbon technologies have increased in performance while decreasing in costs over the past 10 years as many countries have gained significant experience in deployment.[7] Technology choice will depend on the specific status and resources of the country, but there is a strong rationale to use the pandemic recovery period to invest in clean energy technologies.[8] For example, both solar and wind power technologies can often offer long-term cost savings over conventional power production from coal, gas, and oil. Energy efficiency technologies can be deployed to limit increases in energy demand as countries increase in economic prosperity. These rationales provide the impetus for countries to begin investing in clean energy technologies at this time as ongoing performance improvements and cost reductions are expected to increase the value of these technologies further in the future. Investments in conventional pollution control and increased emphasis on technology innovation, with climate change benefits, could be areas of opportunity for investment by DMCs with long-term benefits.[9]

ADB has continued to invest in its DMCs as they struggle to manage during the COVID-19 pandemic and the recovery phase. The need for modernized energy systems is essential to meet the Sustainable Development Goals (SDGs) and ADB will continue to support the low-carbon transition as committed under the Paris Agreement (including reductions of GHGs and other air pollutants). In this respect, ADB's current energy sector operations are well aligned with the needs of DMCs. There is also an opportunity to expand the scope of interventions to address gaps, such as access to electricity and "clean cooking," and to increasingly leverage cross-sector opportunities for DMCs. This focus fits squarely within ADB's mission, and aligns with its Strategy 2030.[10]

---

7 The International Renewable Energy Agency (IRENA) states that from 2010 to 2019, the cost of electricity from solar photovoltaic (PV) has declined by 82%, followed by concentrating solar power at 47%, onshore wind at 40%, and offshore wind at 29%.

8 In 2020, shares of renewable energy in power generation continued to increase, in part due to the completion of projects already in progress at the beginning of the pandemic, and in part due to the competitiveness of the technology compared to fossil fuel-based generation, market structures that support renewables, and the speed projects can be deployed.

9 A central feature of ADB's Healthy Oceans Action Plan is increased investment in onshore solid waste management and other conventional pollution control infrastructure. https://www.adb.org/news/adb-launches-5-billion-healthy-oceans-action-plan.

10 ADB. 2018. Strategy 2030: Achieving a Prosperous, Inclusive, Resilient, and Sustainable Asia and the Pacific. Manila.

The purpose of this note is to (i) highlight the effects of COVID-19 on the energy sector and describe how the sector is responding, (ii) identify key actions that the broad set of energy sector stakeholders[11] can take in both the response and the recovery phase, and (iii) identify the existing strength of ADB's energy sector and how it can respond to the needs of DMCs in light of COVID-19. This note offers guidance on where to maintain ongoing areas of focus and where to place increased focus to address gaps in support of sustainable development in DMCs. Insights shared in this guidance note are expected to be of relevance and interest to stakeholders regionally and internationally as they engage to deliver resilient infrastructure in the Asia and Pacific region and beyond.

This note will focus on the primary areas where ADB invests in the energy sector: (i) power sector—including generation, transmission, and distribution, as well as end use; and (ii) natural gas transmission, distribution, and use—including liquified natural gas (LNG) infrastructure. The next steps following the development of this guidance note will require regional- and country-specific analysis to orient actions that can best address recovery from he pandemic.

---

[11] Energy sector stakeholders include governments, regulators, utilities, end users, financiers, and the private sector.

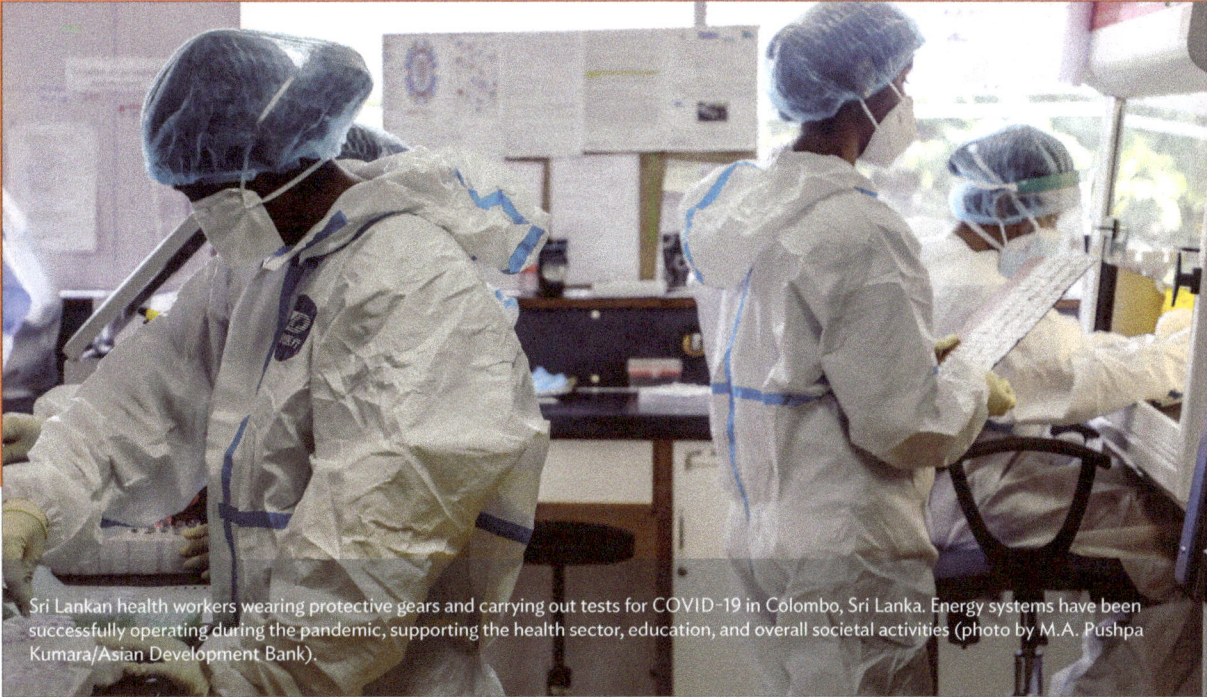

Sri Lankan health workers wearing protective gears and carrying out tests for COVID-19 in Colombo, Sri Lanka. Energy systems have been successfully operating during the pandemic, supporting the health sector, education, and overall societal activities (photo by M.A. Pushpa Kumara/Asian Development Bank).

2 Impacts of COVID-19 on the Global Energy Sector

The global energy sector consists of a highly interrelated set of resources being used for a broad range of end uses that support economic activity and societal well-being. The sector includes a wide range of actors that include public and private sector stakeholders. For example, the power sector uses a range of fuels from fossil-based products (oil, natural gas, coal, or diesel); renewables (photovoltaics, wind, geothermal, hydro); and nuclear for generation. The power that is generated is then distributed through transmission and distribution infrastructure to consumers at different prices depending on the sector (industrial, commercial, or residential). In addition to this, some industry actors produce their own power and some last-mile customers use small-scale individual systems to meet modest power needs. The stakeholders involved in the process can include all levels of governments, utilities, independent regulators, private sector firms, and financiers. While the technical aspects of power generation, transmission, and distribution; and demand, are virtually the same in all countries, the structure of policy, regulation, and wholesale and retail markets varies from country to country.

The demand for energy has dramatically decreased during the initial lockdown periods and the economic effects have resulted in year-on-year decline in 2020. The demand in some countries is recovering, but on a global basis, it is estimated that overall primary energy demand will decrease by over 5% year-on-year in 2020. The decrease in energy demand is much greater in 2020 than any experience in the past 7 decades (Figure 1). This would amount to a shock around seven times larger than that which occurred during the 2007–2008 financial crisis.

Figure 1: Change in Global Primary Energy Demand, 1900–2020e

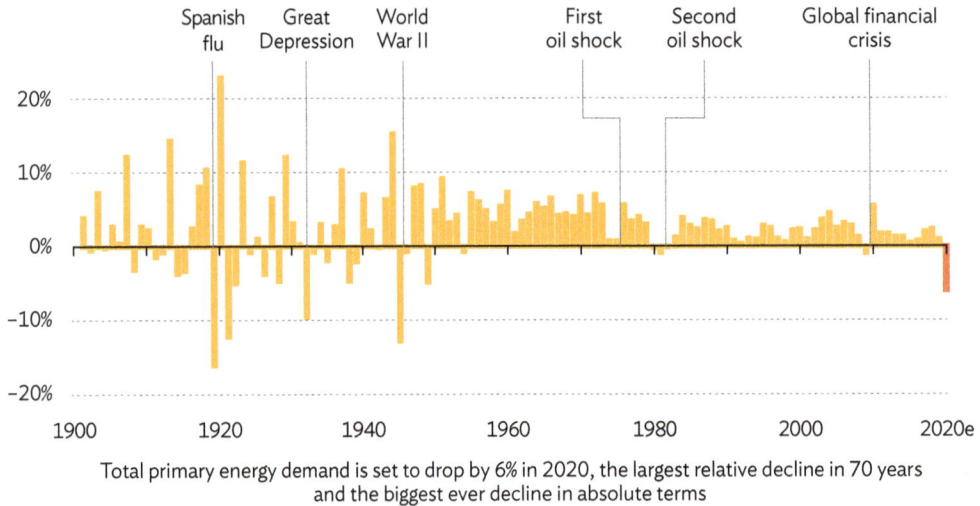

Spanish   Great   World   First   Second   Global financial
flu   Depression War II   oil shock   oil shock   crisis

Total primary energy demand is set to drop by 6% in 2020, the largest relative decline in 70 years
and the biggest ever decline in absolute terms

Note: 2020e = estimated values for 2020.

Source: International Energy Agency (IEA). 2020. Global Energy Review. Paris.

All fuels have experienced decreases in demand, except renewables (Figure 2). The reduction in GHG
emissions is welcome, but is not structural in nature; rather, it is only related to the economic downturn and
reduced transport acitivity during the pandemic. The reductions in energy sector investments will have both
direct economic effects, especially in fossil fuel-producing countries, but also may temporarily halt investment
strategies to enable reorientation toward low-carbon solutions.

**Figure 2: Comparison of Energy Demand, Carbon Dioxide Emissions, and Investment Indicators
(2020, Relative to 2019)**

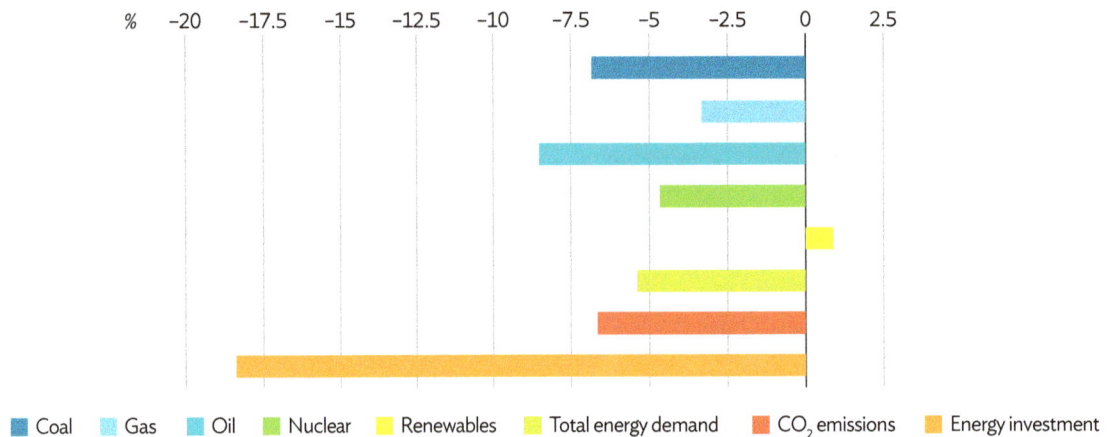

Legend: Coal | Gas | Oil | Nuclear | Renewables | Total energy demand | CO_2 emissions | Energy investment

CO_2 = carbon dioxide.

Source: International Energy Agency (IEA). Key Estimated Energy Demand, CO_2 Emissions and Investment Indicators, 2020 Relative to 2019. Paris.

The decrease in electricity demand is less pronounced at a modest 2% and renewable generation is expected to surpass 2019 levels. This is due to its preferential position in the merit order due to low operating costs, as well as the increased capacity still being constructed and coming on line throughout 2020.

Annual GHG emissions are estimated to decrease by 7% in 2020. According to the Climate Action Tracker, a 4%–11% reduction could occur in 2020, and between 1% above and 9% below 2019 emissions in 2021, depending on the magnitude and length of the economic turndown.[12] However, emissions are likely to rebound fairly quickly, and a short-term increase due to pent-up demand is also possible, based on experience from the global financial crisis.[13] Global GHG emissions fell by 1.2% in 2009; however, the deployment of large stimulus packages was followed by a 5.9% rebound in 2010—well above the long-term average growth in emissions of around 2%.[14]

Global Trends in the Oil and Gas Sectors and Effects on Developing Member Countries

The decline in transport activity during the pandemic has had massive impacts to global oil demand. Global demand in oil decreased by 25% year-on-year in April 2020 largely due to the sharp drop in transport activity both domestic and globally (mobility consumes over 50% of global oil product supply), but also due to reduced demand in industrial sectors. This decrease in global demand, together with other geopolitical factors in oil-producing countries, resulted in major oil price declines on global indexes, to the point where futures prices became negative for the first time in history (if only for a brief period).[15]

As of December 2020, restrictions on various travel modalities continue and there are still significant restrictions in many ADB member countries (Table 1). Global oil prices have recovered, but not to the levels prior to the extensive global lockdowns that limited travel.

Table 1: Overview of Restrictions on Domestic Travel, Urban Public Transit, and International Transport in Selected ADB Member Countries

Country	Transport COVID-19 Policy Status as of December 2020		
	Domestic Travel	**Urban Public Transit**	**International Transport**
Afghanistan	None to limited measures	None to limited measures	Screening arrivals
Australia	Internal movement restricted	None to limited measures	Ban on high-risk region
Azerbaijan	Internal movement restricted	Recommend closing	Total border closure
Bangladesh	Internal movement restricted	Require closing	Ban on high-risk region
Bhutan	Internal movement restricted	Require closing	Ban on high-risk region
Brunei Darussalam	None to limited measures	None to limited measures	Quarantine arrivals
China, People's Republic of	Internal travel restricted	Require closing	Ban on high-risk region

continued on next page

continued on next page

---

[12] Climate Action Tracker. 2020. *A Government Roadmap for Addressing the Climate and Post COVID-19 Economic Crises*. (April update).
[13] ADB. 2020. *Accelerating Climate and Disaster Resilience and Low-Carbon Development through the COVID-19 Recovery: Technical Note*. Manila.
[14] Global Carbon Project. 2011. *Global Emissions Rebound to Record Levels after GFC*. 5 December. Canberra.
[15] For some market perspective, permanent elimination of demand on the order of 10% of global crude oil supply would be equivalent to eliminating almost all of Saudi Arabia's current production.

Table 1 continued

Country	Transport COVID-19 Policy Status as of December 2020		
	Domestic Travel	**Urban Public Transit**	**International Transport**
Fiji	None to limited measures	None to limited measures	Ban on high-risk region
Georgia	Internal movement restricted	Require closing	Ban on high-risk region
India	Recommend not to travel	Recommend closing	Ban on high-risk region
Indonesia	Internal movement restricted	Recommend closing	Ban on high-risk region
Japan	Recommend not to travel	Recommend closing	Total border closure
Kazakhstan	Internal movement restricted	Recommend closing	Ban on high-risk region
Korea, Republic of	Recommend not to travel	None to limited measures	Ban on high-risk region
Kyrgyz Republic	None to limited measures	None to limited measures	Quarantine arrivals
Lao People's Democratic Republic	None to limited measures	None to limited measures	Total border closure
Malaysia	Recommend not to travel	Recommend closing	Ban on high-risk region
Mongolia	Internal travel restricted	Recommend closing	Total border closure
Nepal	Recommend not to travel	Recommend closing	Ban on high-risk region
New Zealand	None to limited measures	None to limited measures	Total border closure
Papua New Guinea	None to limited measures	None to limited measures	Quarantine arrivals
Philippines	Recommend not to travel	Recommend closing	Quarantine arrivals
Singapore	None to limited measures	None to limited measures	Ban on high-risk region
Sri Lanka	Internal travel restricted	Require closing	Ban on high-risk region
Thailand	Internal travel restricted	Recommend closing	Quarantine arrivals
Timor-Leste	Recommend not to travel	None to limited measures	Total border closure
Uzbekistan	None to limited measures	None to limited measures	Ban on high-risk region
Vanuatu	Internal travel restricted	None to limited measures	Total border closure
Viet Nam	None to limited measures	None to limited measures	Total border closure

ADB = Asian Development Bank, COVID-19 = coronavirus disease.
Note: Due to availability, the specific date of data varies from 1–31 December 2020. The latest value available in the month of December is used for all countries. Some restrictions vary across countries.

Source: University of Oxford. Coronavirus Government Response Tracker (accessed 15 January 2021).

The decline in oil prices is a near-term advantage for net-consuming countries. Countries will save money by reducing the cost of providing oil resources to their economies. From a structural perspective, this may limit the motivation to shift to renewables or increase energy efficiency across sectors since the decrease in oil prices will result in lowering the economic advantage of photovoltaic or wind power for electricity generation. In this context, countries may consider retrenchment in fossil-based generation in the near term. This would maintain the risk exposure for countries to oil markets, which are expected to recover in price due to economic recovery or lower production by producers. Second, continuing to rely on imported fossil fuels reduces energy security by depending on nonindigenous fuels where deliveries can also be disrupted by weather-related events.

For oil-producing countries (such as Azerbaijan, Kazakhstan, Turkmenistan, and Viet Nam), this is a negative impact on revenues that could create broad economic challenges in the near term (this also applies to countries producing natural gas such as Papua New Guinea and Uzbekistan). This will mean that these countries have less financial resources available to respond to the health crisis and support recovery initiatives. There is little that can be done in the short term, but in the longer-term perspective, this may provide the political will to ensure that economies are adequately diversified to economically weather such shocks that directly impact the oil and natural gas industries, or potential long-term reductions in demand as countries address climate change.

While a reduction in fossil fuel investments is positive from a climate perspective, it will mean the loss of investments in oil-producing countries and a loss of livelihood for many workers in these industries. In the long term, this could create further price volatility; and likewise in the medium term, if market demand recovers and supply is limited due to a lack of investment.[16] In this context, the countries that take advantage of low prices, but do not shift away from growing their oil demand, will be exposed to price fluctuations in the future.

Demand for natural gas has also decreased, but to a lesser degree than demand for oil and coal. While India, Pakistan, the PRC, and Thailand have all experienced decreases in demand during lockdown periods, it has been less than other developed regions like Europe or North America. These emerging Asian economies have also seen a faster, albeit varied, recovery, and demand is not yet up to 2019 levels on average.

The net decrease in global demand for natural gas has meant that LNG prices on the spot market have decreased significantly, even below historically low levels prior to COVID-19. While much of global gas supplied in Asia is traded on long term oil-indexed pricing[17] (for both LNG and pipeline-supplied gas), some countries are able to take advantage of spot markets if they have not fully locked in regasification terminal capacity to long-term contracts. All the abovementioned developing Asian countries (excluding Pakistan) have significantly increased their imports of LNG compared to the previous year, taking advantage of lower prices and limited domestic consumption. Pakistan has been absent from the LNG spot market and may soon allow third-party access to unused regasification capacity at its import terminals that could support spot market participation, especially in the forthcoming heating season.[18]

While demand for coal is estimated to decrease by nearly 7% globally, most of this decrease was in Europe and North America where coal power generation has not been utilized in favor of lower-cost natural gas. In the PRC, economic recovery resulted in lower decrease in global coal demand as it accounts for more than 50% of coal use worldwide.[19] India decreased its use of coal for power production and utilized lower-cost spot LNG, which supported higher gas burn in India's underutilized gas-fired generation fleet during the peak summer season (footnote 19).

---

[16] International Energy Agency (IEA). 2020. *World Energy Investment 2020*. Paris.
[17] Note that the oil-indexed prices are adjusted with a time lag of 6–9 months and therefore these prices are dropping in the second half of 2020 based on the oil price decreases seen earlier in 2020.
[18] IEA. 2020. *Global Gas Security Review 2020*. Paris.
[19] IEA. 2020. *World Energy Outlook 2020*. Paris.

Power Supply and Demand

Compared to other energy carriers such as oil, natural gas, or coal, electricity itself is not traded globally and is only traded regionally where practical physical interconnections can be established. Power systems across ADB DMCs vary from large nationally interconnected systems that may include regional trade across international borders, to small microgrid systems powerered by diesel generation, or solar home systems providing basic electricity services. Even within countries, urban centers may be largely served by centralized power production delivered by transmission and distribution systems, whereas urban slums, rural, or island communities may have unmet demand or be served by small or micro systems.

In addition to the physical elements of the system, there is a wide range of institutional and governance structures that involve national, regional, and municipal governments; private sector actors; as well as independent regulators. Some systems are still largely supplied and managed by state-owned entities, while others are increasingly moving to private sector participation in parts of the system—especially in generation.

While electricity in itself is not traded globally, core elements of the technology are traded internationally with certain countries taking leadership in manufacturing. The PRC maintains the largest share of solar photovoltaic (PV) manufacturing, whereas Europe and the United States still maintain strong capacities in natural gas turbines and wind turbines.

During lockdowns that have occurred across countries, electricity consumption dropped significantly and patterns of demand throughout the week reflected patterns typically seen only on Sundays.[20] With dramatic reductions in the service and industry sectors, increased residential consumption during this time only partially made up for this loss of demand, resulting in a net decrease.

Detailed power sector data for Asia and Pacific countries is not necessarily available, but some countries have accessible data that provides a snapshot of the effects of COVID-19 lockdowns annually and estimates for the full year in 2020. Total demand for grid electricity in India between 25 March and 24 April in 2020 sharply decreased by around 25% compared to the demand for the same period in 2019.[21] In the Philippines, electricity consumption dropped by around 30% during the Luzon-wide enhanced community quarantine from 15 March to 16 May 2020.[22] In Indonesia, the state electricity corporation Perusahaan Listrik Negara (PLN) is facing a 15% decrease in electricity demand for 2020.

The net result of reductions in electricity demand as well as the decline in industrial operations has reduced demand (and therefore prices) for fuels needed to generate electricity (and for similar fuels that provide energy to industrial processes). As COVID-19 has had effects on a global scale, global demand decreased most for fossil fuels used in the power sector, primarily natural gas and coal, depressing market prices compared to recent trends. While these decreases in fuel prices can provide some benefits to countries, those with utilities locked into take-or-pay contracts were still required to purchase fuels, despite having less requirements. In countries with significant activitiy in the tourism sector, demand for power decreased dramatically due to an almost complete stop in tourism-based travel, but those dependent on fuel imports will be buffered somewhat by the lower commodity prices due to decreasing prices across global markets.

---

[20] Sundays have typically lower power demand compared to other days of the week as there is decreased economic and industrial activity.
[21] M. T. Parray. 2020. *Is Covid-19 An Opportunity To Clean Up India's Coal Power Plants Faster?* 15 June. Brookings.
[22] D. Rivera. 2020. Power Consumption Drops 30% Amid Luzon-side Quarantine. *The Philippine Star*. 22 March.

The share of renewable power, primarily solar and wind, to overall power production increased in 2020. This has been the result of ongoing deployment of projects that had been started prior to the pandemic, and that renewable power is typically the first fuel source dispatched for power production due to its low operating costs (the fuel is generally free).[23] The increasing share of power production from variable renewables has in some cases caused concerns on system stability, but overall, power systems demonstrated excellent technical resilience and operated adequately using higher shares of renewables.

In India, the decrease in electricity demand was almost entirely borne by the coal power plants, with the average coal generation decreasing to 86 gigawatts (GW) between 25 March and 24 April 2020. This accounted for a 29% decrease year-on-year from 116 GW in 2019. The peak instantaneous coal generation in this period was 110 GW, compared to 132 GW for the previous year. On the other hand, renewable energy being "must run," continued to be dispatched at full capacity (footnote 23).

As in other countries, grid power in India generally operated within normal parameters, but some customers experienced increased power cuts during the pandemic. Of the respondents who were part of an ADB phone survey, 15% with grid power and supplemental solar power systems indicated increased outages in grid power between January and June 2020. During this period, more than 85% of the respondents who experienced these outages indicated that solar power helped them manage during the COVID-19 pandemic.[24] This highlights the value of supplemental power supply to increase resilience during a crisis event.

Once lockdown periods were partially relaxed in several countries, electricity demand began to recover, but the amount of recovery has varied widely across countries. In the PRC, where demand for power decreased by 13% in February 2020, demand largely recovered as the lockdown was eased and even exceeded 2019 levels by June. In India, electricity demand has slowly been increasing since the lowest point, and was approaching 2019 levels in August.[25]

Countries that are highly dependent on tourism, such as those in the Pacific, are not expected to rebound so quickly in energy demand as their economies could experience an extended shock. Tourism receipts were estimated to account for up to 20%–30% of economic activity in countries like Samoa and Tonga, and tourism is a prime source of employment and foreign exchange for such countries as Fiji, Palau, and Samoa.[26] In March 2020, a report on Palau projected that tourist arrivals would decrease by over 50% in 2020 compared to 2019 levels, and remain negligible through 2021.[27] COVID-19 has become a new downside risk to utilities in these countries and will be facing two headwinds: drastic decline in power demand and widening gap in liquidity to sustain basic infrastructure.[28]

---

[23] With the exception of biomass, which typically has a fixed feedstock cost. Some hydropower programs include a fee paid to governments for economic use of a river.

[24] As part of Technical Assistance 8993, subproject 2, ADB conducted a phone survey with over 1,600 residential customers who bought solar power systems between August 2019 and January 2020 to supplement grid power in the Indian provinces of Bihar, Odisha, and Uttar Pradesh.

[25] IEA. 2020. *Covid-19 Impact on Electricity*. Paris.

[26] International Monetary Fund. 2020. Pacific Islands Threatened by COVID-19. 27 May

[27] Republic of Palau. 2020. Assessing the Impact of COVID-19 on the Palauan Economy. *EconMAP Technical Note*.

[28] R. Abbasov. 2020. Are Pacific Power Utilities Ready for the Impacts of COVID-19? Asian Development Blog. 8 April.

Financial Impacts for Energy Producers and Utilities

Despite concerns over personnel shortages during lockdowns and limitations on O&M due to travel restrictions, energy system operation and supply was able to continue reliably and meet demand in response to the pandemic.[29]

From a financial perspective, power sector utilities have been severely affected due to the combination of reduced demand for electricity and gas, and reduced payment capability by customers. In some utilities, reduced demand resulted in decreased revenues, but expenses were not reduced due to take-or-pay clauses in fuel or power purchase agreements. In some countries, increasing unemployment due to the pandemic limited the ability of consumers to pay their electricity bills. While some utilities have been able to mitigate fuel supply and power purchase agreements through either force majeure clauses, renegotiating payment terms or government support; decreased demand and payment delays; and delinquency of utility bills by end consumers (residential, commercial, and industrial) are beginning to have a detrimental effect along the energy supply chain. Many governments have intervened by maintaining electricity services to the population during the lockdown, while also reducing the negative financial impact on the sector.[30] Since many utilities were already under financial stress prior to the crisis, the pandemic is further deteriorating the financial health of these organizations.

Some analysts have projected that annual losses of Indian distribution companies will, as a result of the pandemic, double to about $15 billion and result in the delay or cancellation of new investments. In response to COVID-19, India is demonstrating a mix of policy announcements that indicate financial stress as well as trying to continue with electricity system development, for example:

    (i) Deadlines for commissioning of generation projects extended; the Ministry of New and Renewable Energy confirmed extensions for the duration of the April lockdown plus 30 days for renewable power projects (treated as force majeure).

    (ii) The Ministry of New and Renewable Energy also declared "must run" status of renewable projects and ordered distribution companies to pay generators. Still, some relaxation of payments has been allowed, a signal of persistent distribution company financial stress.

    (iii) Some state governments are also allowing payment delays by consumers on electricity bills.

    (iv) Continuation of solar reverse auctions (a tender for a 2 GW solar PV project was finalized on 16 April 2020 with an off-take price of $34/megawatt-hour).

    (v) The government has put in place measures to boost power sector investment, particularly private capital (e.g., extending participation of nonfinancial banking companies, launching a new investment fund and improving bankability of power purchase agreements).[31]

As highlighted above, the PLN in Indonesia is facing a 15% decrease in electricity demand in 2020, while the depreciation of the Indonesian rupiah has increased the cost of US dollar-priced electricity generation by $533 million. Combined, these reduced PLN's revenue growth to 1.6% and profits by 96.0% to $17.4 million in the first half of 2020 compared with $506 million in 2019. In its efforts to respond to these adverse developments, PLN reduced its fuel cost by 15.5%, personnel cost by 19.8%, and planned investments by 50.0%.[32]

---

[29] Power system balance of supply and demand can be challenging during both periods of increased and decreased demand, especially when high shares of variable renewables are prioritized for dispatch during low-demand periods, increasing the share of non-dispatchable variable generation.

[30] International Finance Corporation. 2020. *The Impact of COVID-19 on the Power Sector*.

[31] IEA. 2020. *World Energy Investment 2020*. Paris.

[32] Indonesia Energy Sector Assessment, Strategy, and Road Map – Update 2020.

In the Philippines, the reliance on imported coal and decreased demand for electricity during COVID-19 put consumers at risk of financial costs due to take-or-pay contracts. The country's largest utility, Meralco, invoked force majeure clauses in its supply contracts in response to the COVID-19 crisis and therefore consumers were prevented from a 15% increase in electricity rates to cover the costs of the coal contracts. In contrast, electric cooperatives have been largely unable to trigger force majeure negotiations because of their small size, lack of negotiating power, and reliance on nonstandard contracts. The only option electric cooperatives can take to protect low-income households who rely on them for power is to request the waiver of the minimum energy off-take provision.[33]

Rural populations are typically the focus for off-grid energy, but there are also those within urban centers who lack access to grid power. While different in context, both of these populations have experienced challenges during the pandemic that are similar as they are typically served with basic energy solutions like solar home systems and clean cookstoves. Companies and nongovernment organizations that have established pay-as-you-go solar home system business models may still require in-person payment. Many of these suppliers have allowed energy services to be provided without payment during lockdowns, but this has caused financial stress to project developers in this segment. In one survey covering Africa, Asia, and Latin America, 85% of the companies are struggling with survival beyond a period of more than 5 months. Small companies (e.g., distributors) are especially more severely affected by the crisis. The crisis has reached a critical stage for most of the companies, with severe effects on employment and ultimately on livelihoods. Thirty-five percent of companies had laid off 30% of their staff by July 2020; and additional staff would be potentially laid off in the next few months if no immediate support is available.[34]

Project Deployment and Supply Chain Effects

The renewable energy sector has experienced disruptions to supply chains as a result of the pandemic.[35] In early 2020, many solar PV developers in Asia and other parts of the world have experienced protracted delays in importing solar PV modules and other supplies. According to the International Renewable Energy Agency (IRENA), 50 leading solar PV panel manufacturers maintain factories in 23 countries, with the PRC accounting for about two-thirds of global production in 2018. COVID-19 has interrupted the growth of solar power in some developing countries, where the implementation of solar projects has been affected because international experts and managers have been unable to report for work due to travel restrictions.

Wind power technology has a much more globally interconnected supply chain with significant manufacturing in Europe. Early in 2020, certain parts made in the PRC were facing delays and as the pandemic spread and restrictions in Europe began to have an impact, with closures in Italy and Spain. Manufacturing of components in India were also disrupted during the lockdowns, resulting in delays in markets and with concerns worldwide due to uncertainty in how long lockdowns would last.[36]

Renewable energy value chains also involve technical services such as design, engineering, installation, and O&M. In this regard, a serious skills gap exists in many developing countries in Asia and the Pacific, making them dependent on foreign consultants and contractors to implement projects.

---

[33] S. J. Ahmed and A. Dalusung III. 2020. Philippines Meralco Carve-out Clause Means Power Companies, Investors, Bear the Risk of Ignoring Clean Energy. Institute for Energy Economics and Financial Analysis. 17 August.

[34] Energising Development. 2020. COVID-19 Energy Access Industry Barometer.

[35] This section includes excerpts from an ADB blog focused on solar energy. Additions on other renewable technologies have been added. A full version of the blog can be found at: https://blogs.adb.org/pandemic-may-break-value-chains-but-solar-energy-can-still-shine.

[36] IEA. 2020. The Coronavirus Pandemic Could Derail Renewable Energy's Progress. Government Can Help. Paris.

Energy efficiency and small-scale distributed renewable energy deployments could be the hardest-hit due to lockdown conditions. Both these areas require increased interaction with customers, often at residences. This increases the potential for exposure to COVID-19 to installers and technicians, and therefore limitations while the virus is not yet under control will be significant.

As renewable energy, energy efficiency services, and efficient appliance markets continue to grow, momentum is slowly building for developing countries to consider local manufacturing and support technical capacity. For example, in the solar sector there is interest in the PRC and in some major solar manufacturing countries to relocate part of their production capacity, given their surplus output, rising labor costs, and tensions owing to trade imbalances. The PRC—with about 150 GW per year of solar manufacturing capacity, an amount that is more than the current global demand—has already started to relocate some of this capacity in neighboring countries such as India and Viet Nam. There has been a renewed push for "Make in India," a central government program to boost domestic manufacturing and create jobs.[37]

Other developing countries should also consider similar strategies to join part of the low-carbon value chain, at least to assemble solar modules, mounting structures, and other nonproprietary aspects, as well as O&M. If developing a domestic manufacturing industry for technologies is hindered by a limited local market, several options can be explored. These options include forming a joint venture among neighboring countries that will put up subregional manufacturing hubs.

---

[37] R. Tongia. 2020. How COVID-19 Might Impact India's Renewal Energy Transition. World Economic Forum. 19 May.

Single water discharge for hydropower plant in Tajikistan. Regional and national resources need to be consider for sustainable energy sector development (photo by Nozim Kalandarov/Asian Development Bank).

3 Guidance for Energy Sector Response and Recovery in the COVID-19 Context

There is significant uncertainty as to how long the health issues of the pandemic will remain or how countries will choose to manage recovery, making economic and energy demand projections highly uncertain. The once-in-a-century nature of the pandemic is causing massive economic effects, but lack of clarity on the magnitude of effects and what the "new normal" will look like for society means that specific planning is fraught with uncertainty.

There is a need for "no regrets" development planning in the energy sector that meets the near-term needs of societies and continues to address long-term priorities. Despite tremendous progress over the last 40 years in Asia and the Pacific, there remains over 230 million people without access to electricity and nearly 1.7 billion people without access to clean cooking.[38] While the future resolution of the COVID-19 pandemic remains uncertain, there is agreement on the need for energy access to support the development needs in Asia and the Pacific, and how energy investments need to support climate change mitigation and adaptation. These priorities remain consistent since prior to COVID-19 and projects within the energy sector can also directly support economic recovery.

[38] IEA. 2020. *SDG7: Data and Projections. Paris*.

End-Use Sector Demand Trends during Response and Recovery

Mobility restrictions in response to COVID-19 have resulted in drastic changes in travel behavior. Swift lockdowns across the globe have forced many nonessential workers to work from home almost overnight, and schools to shift to e-learning. With the closure of brick-and-mortar shops and restaurants during the containment period, consumers have flocked to online shopping and food delivery. The sharp reductions in economic activity have also curbed regional and national freight transport activity. Urban freight and logistics, on the other hand, have prospered in many places because of the increased online shopping and food deliveries.[39]

The shifts in energy demand across sectors throughout 2020 has now been documented quite well. While the future use of energy is not fully predictable, several structural shifts could occur in the medium term (Table 2). Increased working from home, which has been a necessity during the response phase, may well continue into the recovery phase. This has an effect on several aspects of energy use: increased residential consumption, decreased transport activity, and decreased energy consumption in office spaces.

Demand for energy in large-scale industrial sectors decreased during the lockdown periods, but demand in some industries largely recovered when lockdowns were eased. The longer-term return to pre-pandemic outputs will be much more dependent on global, regional, and national economic recovery as countries move beyond focusing primarily on health measures.

Table 2: Energy Demand Trends

Sector	During Response Phase	During Recovery Phase	Medium-Term Behavioral Change or Sector Shift
Transport			
• Personal Transport	↓	↑	↓
• Public Transport	↓	↓	→ ↓ ↑ ?
• Air Travel	↓	↓	↓
• Urban Freight and Logistics	↑	→ ↑	→ ↑
Residential Buildings	↑	↑	↑
ICI Buildings			
• Health	↑	↑	↑
• Service/ Retail	↓	↓	↓
• Education	↓	↓	→ ↑ ↓ ?
• Office/Government	↓	↓	→ ↑ ↓ ?
• Information Technology	↑	↑	↑
• Tourism	↓	↓	
Large- and Medium-Scale Industry	↓	↓	→ ↑ ↓ ?

COVID-19 = coronavirus disease; ICI = institutional, commercial, and industrial.
Notes:
1. Medium-term projections are highly uncertain in light of health, economic, and sectoral uncertainties. Long-term considerations are not considered in the figure. Parts of the table with more than one trend indicator demonstrates areas that are either uncertain or can differ significantly from country to country.
2. Several trends experienced during the COVID-19 pandemic have accelerated and already underway, i.e., shift from retail to online, increased videoconferencing, overall digitization, etc.

Source: Asian Development Bank staff assessment.

---

[39] ADB. 2020. *Guidance Note on COVID-19 and Transport in Asia and the Pacific*. Manila. 24 July.

There are several specific areas of particular uncertainty. In many countries, the demand for public transport has significantly reduced due to either government shutdown of services, space requirements, or due to health concerns from passengers. In this context, if there is a desire to deliver public transport services with social distancing measures in place, the amount of energy used could increase. At the same time, if travel is required, those who can afford personal transport will be inclined to take cars to avoid contact with others. The same can be said for office space. Some organizations may lease additional space to enable in-office occupancy with social distancing. All public spaces, including schools, offices, or mall, could also see increased energy demand if ventilation (to help increase air circulation) is dramatically increased without improvements to efficiency and heat–cool recovery.

Despite uncertainty in planning, the overall strategic priorities for the energy sector can be summarized by separating the initial response to COVID-19 from support required for recovery phase (which by necessity overlaps with the initial response phase), toward long-term sustainable new normal. Key actions for DMCs are highlighted in Figure 3. The wide range of stakeholders in the energy sector will have specific roles to be carried out and are identified in Tables 3 and 5.

Figure 3: Overview of Response and Recovery Actions for ADB Developing Member Countries

Response Phase

- Keep end-user sectors supplied with energy
- Provide financial support to ensure continued operations
- Capture knowledge, identify any scarcity of flexibility resources

Recovery Phase

- Enhance sustainable energy services
- Improve energy sector resilience and security
- Accelerate energy access to the poor and vulnerable
- Apply advanced technology and cross-sector interventions

Source: Asian Development Bank.

Response Phase

During the response phase, key focus is placed on maintaining energy sector operations to supply end-use sectors. Energy stakeholders across DMCs have generally responded well during this phase, and the energy system has technically remained resilient. Hospitals were able to operate sufficiently with respect to their energy needs, and populations were able to work from home and utilize available Information and technology (ICT) resources. In many countries, utilities and consumers have been offered financial support to ensure continued operation of electricity systems, as well as access to electricity and other fuels for consumers despite the initial economic effects of the pandemic.

During the response phase, operating energy systems reliably using a higher share of variable renewables provides a useful case for future system development. It is important for utilities and system operators to identify any scarcity of resources to determine further investments that could provide additional flexibility to operate with higher shares of variable renewable generation, and to increase resilience to other potential disruptions to power systems.

Since the initial effects of COVID-19 still persist in some countries and/or subsequent large-scale lockdowns may still happen, the response phase remains relevant for DMCs. During this phase, it is essential that all stakeholders focus on keeping the energy system operating reliably as this will support not only continued health response to the pandemic, but can also help to minimize economic effects by enabling industries and businesses to continue their operations.

Table 3: Energy Sector Strategic Priorities in the Response to COVID-19

Response to COVID-19	Stakeholder Action
Keep the end-use sectors supplied with energy, responding to changes in overall demand and ability to pay by utilities and end users.	**DMC Governments** ⦿ Prepare for short-term financial support to maintain liquidity of essential actors, primarily utilities for power and natural gas, due to decreased demand and end-user limitations to make payments. ⦿ Monitor market prices of imported fuel and consider subsidy swaps to reduce Treasury costs of imports and reallocate savings to support poor and vulnerable groups. ⦿ Provide energy subsidy to poor and vulnerable groups most economically affected by lockdowns, particularly households headed by women. ⦿ Encourage or stipulate flexibility for timing of deployment for existing projects delayed by travel and social distancing restrictions due to COVID-19. ⦿ Prepare for vaccine rollout and energy supply for cold chain requirements. Consider equipment needs and solar energy use especially in rural or remote areas. **Energy Utilities** ⦿ Maintain technical operation of energy systems to ensure power supply, especially for the health sector and residential residential users where increased demand has been identified. ⦿ Capture know-how and operating procedures from lockdown system operation. These procedures may be needed during subsequent waves of COVID-19 and can provide inputs into future system design for resilience. ⦿ Develop operation protocols to address COVID-19 safety for all employees with special focus on essential employees needed for operations and maintenance. ⦿ Identify key changes in revenue (including both demand reduction and end-user payment limitations) and create strategies to manage finances under changing revenue scenario. ⦿ Adjust and manage infrastructure and maintenance project delivery deadlines due to COVID-19 delays, identifying and prioritizing essential maintenance for reliability. ⦿ Determine energy needs for vaccine delivery, especially in rural and remote regions. Start early and prepare infrastructure required to encourage smooth rollout of vaccines when available. Utilize preparations to also improve health clinic energy services, as appropriate.

continued on next page

Table 3 continued

Response to COVID-19	Stakeholder Action
	Regulators ◉ Capture available data on the effects of pollutants on public health (sanitation, hygiene, solid waste disposal, particulate matter, nitrogen oxide, sulfur oxide, etc.). ◉ Consider tariff adjustments to ensure affordable energy access to all customer segments including marginalized households headed by women. ◉ Instruct utilities to apply "no disconnection" policy during the pandemic.
	Financiers ◉ Provide financing to governments, utilities, or projects under the COVID-19 context. ◉ Adjust financing schedules to support ongoing projects.
	End users ◉ Limit nonessential use of energy if there are payment concerns in order to limit debt. ◉ Access stimulus/emergency funding to continue use of energy for essential needs. ◉ Operate centralized air conditioners under "safe mode" to increase ventilation in public buildings.
	Private Sector ◉ Prepare for rapid deployment of energy technologies and services as needed with focus on health sector and ICT infrastructure. ◉ Determine delivery and deployment processes and procedures considering COVID-19 precautions.

COVID-19 = coronavirus disease, DMC = developing member country, ICT = information and communication technology.
Note: Stakeholders highlighted as DMC governments include the executing agencies and implementing agencies that the Asian Development Bank engages with to deliver technical assistance and loan projects.

Source: Asian Development Bank.

Recovery through Rejuvenation and Resilience

As activity shifts from initial response mode to economic recovery mode, DMCs have both a tremendous challenge and opportunity. The energy sector is shifting due to a range of global trends in technology and markets as well as global commitments to address climate change. Economic recovery provides an opportunity to reconsider development plans to take advantage of recent technological progress, and to make adjustments to become more resilient to market, climate, and other risks, including future pandemics. Second, as the economic stresses that COVID-19 has imparted on many countries, stimulus funding spent on reviving economies must strive to leverage benefits and a broader range of development goals.

COVID-19 is not the first event to impact Asia and the Pacific as well as on a global scale. There can be significant learning from previous crises and how recovery was structured to address effects. The characteristics of successful stimulus interventions to support economic recovery of economies include:
   (i) able to generate jobs and stimulate economic activity, and may involve actions with a short implementation timeline, so that the stimulus funds can be quickly deployed and people can get back to work in a timely manner;
   (ii) labor-intensive, particularly in the early stages;
   (iii) promoting skills development, with objectives such as reskilling unemployed workers from sectors that have been heavily affected by COVID-19, or preparing for a low-carbon future;
   (iv) strong supply chain, which could include considerations such as more localized or more diversified sourcing; and
   (v) high economic multipliers.[40]

---

[40] ADB. 2020. *Accelerating Climate and Disaster Resilience and Low-Carbon Development Through the COVID-19 Recovery*. Manila.

Within the energy sector, there are numerous interventions that can meet the above characteristics and ongoing development needs along with global efforts to align with the Paris Agreement (building upon existing nationally determined contributions as a starting point) and the United Nations SDGs.

Renewable energy deployments and energy efficiency programs can offer significant employment during construction and implementation. While some technologies such as PV panels and power electronics may be manufactured predominantly by only a few countries, balance-of-systems components and assembly can be accomplished in many countries. While capacity building may be needed for the design and deployment of sustainable energy technologies, this can be used to support the development of micro, small, and medim-sized enterprises (MSMEs) that can be part of economic recovery. Together, energy sector interventions provide options to support economic recovery by ensuring a reliable supply of sustainable energy and at the same time act as an economic stimulus through investments and job creation.

Countries with fossil fuel subsidies could take the opportunity at this time to lessen subsidies and align in-country prices with global markets—especially for consumer products such as diesel and gasoline.[41] Oil product subsidies account for billions of dollars per year spent by governments (Table 4) and often the benefits of such subsidies are not well targeted to poor and vulnerable populations. But such actions would need to be carefully balanced during this time where consumers may be under economic pressure, but there could be opportunities to better align subsidies to the benefit of those who need it most. If subsidies are decreased for oil products, they could be oriented to other parts of the energy sector—such as lower prices for electricity—often referred to as subsidy swaps.

Table 4: Annual Subsidies for Oil in Select ADB Developing Member Countries
($ million)

Country	2016	2017	2018	2019
Azerbaijan	273.1	740.8	1,131.1	977.4
China, People's Republic of	15,439.7	18,069.4	17,519.5	18,091.6
India	15,832.8	18,471.1	23,085.1	20,977.2
Indonesia	4,146.0	11,114.1	22,649.5	19,217.7
Kazakhstan	1,773.6	1,848.3	2,882.3	3,050.6
Malaysia	1,511.5	2,029.2	1,803.3	1,811.6
Pakistan	83.7	96.2	108.4	155.8
Sri Lanka	70.5	179.5	188.1	315.4
Thailand	581.7	912.0	913.4	539.6
Turkmenistan	1,034.5	1,513.0	1,351.8	983.7
Uzbekistan	23.7	127.9	441.8	275.3

Source: International Energy Agency. Fossil Fuel Subsidy Database. https://www.iea.org/topics/energy-subsidies (accessed 19 April 2021).

---

[41] It should be noted that subsidies are also given for gas, coal, and electricity.

Job creation (or preserving existing jobs) will be a key part of economic recovery from the pandemic. Investments in the energy sector can support overall economic development and provide energy needed for businesses, industry, and social services in DMCs, but energy projects can also provide job opportunities directly during the recovery phase, providing livelihoods during implementation of projects.

In 2019, approximately 40 million people were employed in the global energy industry; it is estimated that nearly 8 million of these jobs have been lost or are at risk of being lost due to the effects of COVID-19.[42] Efforts to save these jobs is an important consideration in recovery approaches, but an approach that works to accelerate the energy sector development in support of the Paris Agreement and SDGs can also increase employment opportunities. This approach is supported by analysis that indicates that job creation per dollar invested in the renewable sector creates almost three times as many jobs as those in the fossil fuel industry.[43]

During the recovery phase, the energy industry can help stimulate economic activity through construction and manufacturing jobs. The International Energy Agency (IEA) has developed a sustainable recovery scenario that focuses on the deployment of infrastructure in the power sector (generation and grid infrastructure); energy efficiency buildings and industry sectors; manufacturing of vehicles and other transport measures; as well as fuel production, renewables, recycling, and innovation (Figure 4). This scenario is projected to create more than 9 million jobs per year over 3 years from 2021 to 2023.

Figure 4: Annual Average Construction and Manufacturing Jobs Created in the International Energy Agency Sustainable Recovery Plan

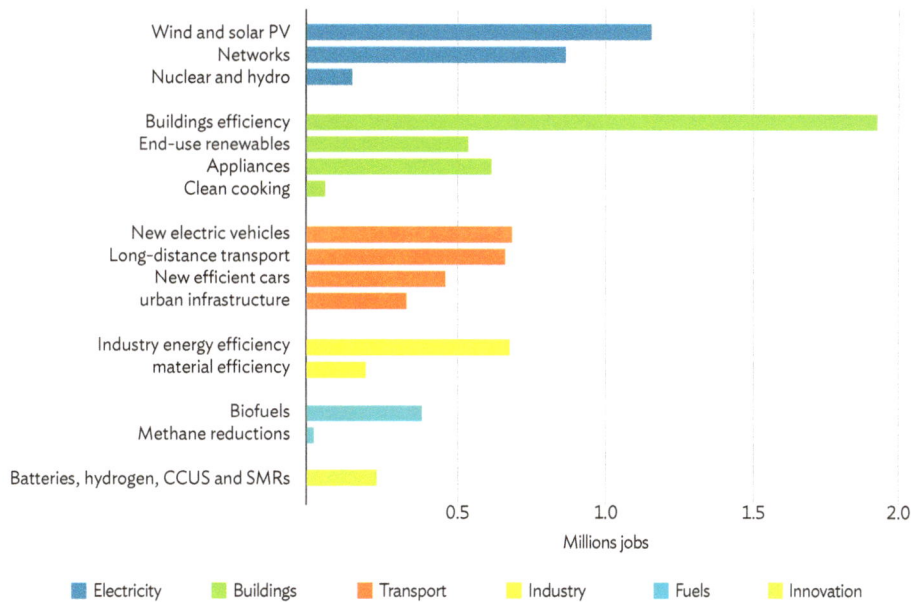

CCUS = carbon capture, utilization, and storage; PV = photovoltaic, SMR = steam methane reforming.

Source: International Energy Agency. 2020. Sustainable Recovery: World Energy Outlook Special Report. Paris.

---

[42] IEA. 2020. Sustainable Recovery: World Energy Outlook Special Report. Paris. The "energy industry" encompasses all supply of fuels to end uses, including the production, transformation, and provision of solid, liquid, and gaseous fuels to consumers, together with the power sector, including the operation, development, and manufacturing of power generation technologies, networks, and storage.
[43] IRENA. 2020. Renewable Energy and Jobs – Annual Review 2020. Abu Dhabi.

While jobs are only permanent if projects continue to be developed, a small share (estimated at 500,000 jobs) will become permanent for O&M. The other jobs will only remain if additional projects are planned and deployed after the 3-year period. But this is consistent with projections that job opportunities will be created by the transition of the energy system to align with global clean energy and climate change goals. While this transition will reduce jobs in in the fossil fuel sector, it will create employement in other sectors to a much greater degree, resulting in a net increase of over 15 million jobs globally by 2030 (Figure 5).

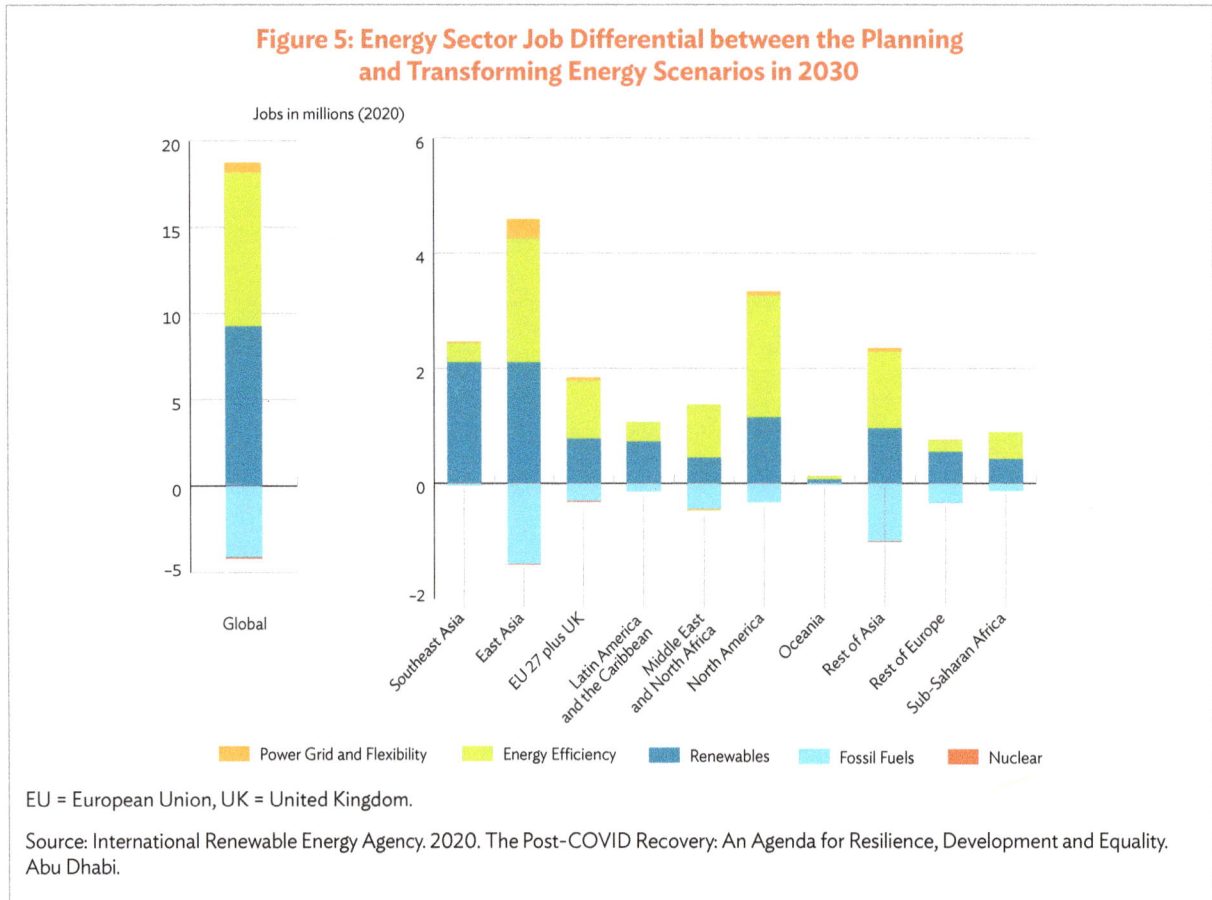

Figure 5: Energy Sector Job Differential between the Planning and Transforming Energy Scenarios in 2030

EU = European Union, UK = United Kingdom.

Source: International Renewable Energy Agency. 2020. The Post-COVID Recovery: An Agenda for Resilience, Development and Equality. Abu Dhabi.

In developing countries, energy efficiency measures will focus much more on using best-in-class technologies during construction of new infrastructure (compared to a much greater focus on renovations in developed countries) as energy sector and energy using base infrastructure (such as buildings and transport) expand rapidly. Moreover, developing countries often have higher employment multipliers compared to developed countries, and therefore investments will result in higher job creation numbers per dollar invested.[44] In low-income countries without full electricity access where many people rely on the traditional use of biomass for cooking, investment in electricity grids, decentralized systems, and clean cooking solutions could employ around 350,000 people globally on average in the period to 2023.[45] This indicates the value of using the stimulus funds to recover from

---

[44] M. Ram et al. 2020. Job creation during the global energy transition towards 100% renewable power system by 2050. *Technological Forecasting and Social Change*. Volume 151, February 2020.
[45] IEA. 2020. *Sustainable Recovery*. June. Paris.

COVID-19 to support a sustainable energy development plan that can kickstart and accelerate the clean energy development in DMCs.

There are also opportunities to support gender equality through a green and low-carbon recovery in the energy sector. In 2019, women represented 32% of full-time employees in the renewable energy sector, compared to 22% in the conventional oil and gas business.[46] This is a positive development and with continued effort these jobs can be safeguarded for women.[47] In the area of providing access to energy, the Solar Mama project by Barefoot College, founded in India, trains women to design and deploy solar home systems, with programs in Africa, Asia, and Latin America. These women, who are mostly illiterate, become solar technicians—bringing clean power and light to their villages. According to the India-based nongovernment organization, every woman electrifies 50 homes on average in her village. By catalyzing employment, boosting income, and providing self-reliant solutions, the initiative works toward several of the SDGs, including No Poverty, Gender Equality, and Affordable and Clean Energy.[48]

The recovery phase presents an opportunity to accelerate progress in energy sector development, and especially in areas that have traditionally not progressed enough such as addressing air pollution, GHG emission, and access to energy. Progress in the energy sector can be part of a holistic approach to a low-carbon and resilient recovery. The recovery phase can be framed as "Recovery through Rejuvenation and Resilience" and can focus on the following four priorities in DMCs:

   (i)   enhancing sustainable energy services (including renewable energy and energy efficiency) to businesses, public services (e.g., health, education) and homes;
   (ii) improving energy sector resilience and security;
   (iii) accelerating energy access to the poor and vulnerable, particularly for clean cooking; and
   (iv) applying advanced technology and cross-sector interventions.

Enhancing sustainable energy services is an ongoing development imperative, but has become more urgent during the pandemic. Most ADB DMCs experience some level of energy inadequacy, from high levels of unmet demand to high annual outage levels, as well as regional disparities within countries. Renewable energy deployments—especially for solar and wind—can now produce power that is cheaper than coal and gas in many countries, providing the economic motivation to deploy these technologies to harvest indigenous renewable resources. Alongside the growth of renewable technology deployment, strong and robust electricity grids will also be needed (footnote 20). ADB is well-placed to support these investments that may otherwise prove to be a weak link in the transformation of the power sector, with implications on the reliability and security of electricity supply. Aligning these investments with COVID-19 recovery stimulus can leverage on development progress while meeting climate goals, and set the stage for ensuring energy infrastructure is well in place for the cold chain needed for COVID-19 vaccine delivery.

Improving energy sector resilience and security has been clearly identified as a need during the COVID-19 pandemic. Although the energy systems have operated well so far, concerns over reliance on international access to skills and capabilities, technologies, and fuel resources mean that energy systems have been put at risk. Renewable energy technologies, when manufactured as well as those deployed and maintained locally, where

---

[46] IRENA. 2019. *Renewable Energy: A Gender Perspective*. Abu Dhabi.
[47] This could be done through parental leave and flexible work hours, equal wages, childcare support, and equal opportunities for professional advancement; and challenging cultural and social norms.
[48] B. Magistretti. 2019. *These "Solar Mamas" Are Trained As Engineers To Bring Power And Light To Their Villages. Forbes.* 25 July.

practical, create resilient energy generation that uses indigenous energy resources. While COVID-19 has reduced the cost of imported fossil fuels, the next shock or crisis could result in limited access or spikes in global fossil fuel prices (as seen in the past), and therefore reduction in the use of imported fuels increases resilience against possible (or probable) future events. Moreover, increased use of ICT across energy infrastructure will require a focus on cybersecurity to ensure that such use of advanced technologies does not introduce other security vulnerabilities.

Looking at broader and long-term resilience and security beyond the current focus during the pandemic, physical climate risks have not disappeared. Energy sector investments need to consider potential physical impacts on infrastructure due to climate change. Investments must also ensure that infrastructure aligns with current and future climate policy and is not stranded, resulting in wasted efforts and resources.

Accelerating energy access to the poor and vulnerable, particularly for clean cooking, has been identified as an urgent response to the pandemic. As a result of the economic effects from COVID-19, the IEA estimates that more than 110 million people, mostly in developing Africa and Asia, could lose their ability to pay for basic electricity services. Initial research indicates that indoor air pollution, such as that due to a lack of access to clean cooking technology, can increase susceptibility to more severe effects of COVID-19.[49] During recovery stimulus, money for pro-poor and pro-vulnerable tariff structures and energy infrastructure can be prioritized to support basic services and productive use of energy. Interventions that focus on small businesses, education, and health will be essential to support populations that have been cut off from overseas-based work opportunities due to COVID-19, ensuring that the next generation does not fall behind in education, and strengthening the health system to address current pandemic-related and future health needs. Accelerating efforts could also focus on existing gaps such as programs that support women-headed households or women-led MSMEs, taking into account that lower income of women has not been adequately addressed in the past.

Applying advanced technology and cross-sector interventions is essential to link the three abovementioned priorities. Along with rapid growth of solar, wind, and energy efficiency technologies, the IEA's Sustainable Development Scenario also emphasizes that the next 10 years will require major scaling up of hydrogen and carbon capture, utilization and storage, and new momentum behind nuclear power, particularly with small modular reactors (footnote 20). Remote management and payment systems can enable access to energy in last-mile applications essential for cold chain infrastructure needed for vaccine deployment. Automated metering infrastructure can reduce contact between people for billing purposes to help limit the spread of COVID-19, while reducing commercial losses for utilities. Battery storage systems can increase the efficiency of system operation and support renewable integration. Cross-sector interventions can include modern and clean waste-to-energy systems that can safely address increased medical waste during COVID-19 response, while providing needed energy supply. Providing energy to telecommunication towers, schools, and health clinics as anchor loads to mini-grids that can be then extended to communities and small businesses are practical cross-sector interventions. These are just a small set of examples that can be deployed to support countries in meeting the first three priorities as their economies recover from the pandemic.

While the timing for recovery of overall energy demand is not certain, many countries have demonstrated that electricity demand has been the fastest to recover (footnote 43). In developing countries, the power sector is typically in need of rejuvenation, modernization, and expansion in order to serve the growing needs of society and low-carbon transition. From this perspective, the power sector will be a very important sector in which to invest. Moreover, the sector will continue to have a role addressing COVID-19, such as enabling high-quality medical

---

[49] A. Karan et al. 2020. The impact of air pollution on the incidence and mortality of COVID-19. *Global Health Research and Policy vol.* 5.

care; developing the cold chain for vaccine delivery when available; as well as supporting education, building ventilation in cities, and improving many aspects of modern life.

Countries in colder climates (such as Central and West Asian countries, Mongolia, and Nepal, as well as parts of India and the PRC) need to consider actions beyond the power sector, and may have increased emphasis on other fuels and energy technologies such as geothermal, heat pumps, and natural gas. Renewable energy technologies in the heating sector are less financially viable at this stage and may require added financial support. In addition, natural gas can play an important role, especially for heating and cooking, to shift away from unsustainable use of bioenergy and coal-based technologies.

The decline in air pollution due to decreased transport activity during lockdowns has clearly highlighted the need to develop low-carbon transport systems. The concept of avoid–shift–improve, used in the transport sector, highlights the need for urban planning along with a focus on technology. Urban planning and development can further reduce transport activity, i.e., establishing workplaces near residential areas to minimize commuting or by improving ICT infrastructure to accommodate work-from-home arrangements. Urban planning can also support a low-carbon approach by including nonmotorized modes of transport in the design of roads (e.g., bike lanes and walking lanes) and public transit infrastructure. In parallel, policies that encourage the adoption of higher fuel and efficiency standards or the use of electric vehicles will help reduce vehicle emissions.

The development of low-carbon transport infrastructure is more easily accommodated in modern urban developments, but significant progress can also be accomplished in other citiies. The Xiangtan Low-Carbon Transformation Sector Development Program, for example, will help the municipal government transform public transport through 60 kilometers of dedicated bus lanes with transit signal priority, real-time bus information, better access to walking and cycling lanes, improved access at two railway stations, and improved road safety in school zones.[50]

Beyond technical considerations, stakeholders in the energy sector must work together to ensure strong support for recovery from the pandemic. A major part of this is the policy and regulatory environment to support sustainable energy technologies such as a robust legal environment, transparent procurement and tender processes, and sustainable tariffs leading to the financial viability of utilities. Without strong governance in the sector, it will be more difficult to attract and engage the private sector across investment, design, and deployment.

The actions highlighted in Table 5 offer a broad range of aspects that must be addressed. These are meant to be comprehensive in an overarching manner, but it is expected that new and additional opportunities for energy sector development exist in specific country contexts. Moreover, not all actions will apply to all countries at the same time or at all, but rather this provides a menu that can be considered and used to address the most needed or most beneficial priorities as part of the recovery process, while preparing for future investments. Some may be considered near-term priorities, whereas to other countries, they may be considered as long-term actions built upon other near-term actions.

---

[50] ADB. 2020. $200 Million in ADB Loans to Demonstrate a Low-Carbon and Resilient City Growth Model in Xiangtan, PRC. News release. 13 October.

Table 5: Energy Sector Priorities in the Recovery from COVID-19

Recovery through Rejuvenation and Resilience	Stakeholder Action
Enhance energy service to businesses; public services (e.g., health, education, waste, transport); and homes that address air quality issues (particulate matter, nitrogen oxide, sulfur oxide); is low-carbon, affordable, and reliable.	**DMC Governments** ⊘ Create clean, just, and low-carbon road map for the energy sector development through multistakeholder engagement, aligned with commitments under the Paris Agreement that address the needs of industrial, institutional, commercial, and residential sectors. ⊘ Align interventions with nationally determined contributions to the Paris Agreement. ⊘ Utilize energy sector development, particularly renewable energy deployments, as an economic development and job creation platform for recovery from the pandemic. ⊘ Develop sector governance environment with specific and tailored transparent regulations, utilizing both state-owned and private sector approaches, as appropriate. ⊘ Determine policy mix to meet long-term clean and low-carbon energy goals (country specific), for example: • price carbon emissions and other pollutants; • create full-cost recovery energy tariffs that encourage energy efficiency alongside lifeline tariffs for vulnerable groups; • create renewable energy portfolio mix targets and enabling environment to meet targets including private sector engagement; • develop and deploy programs on demand-side energy efficiency including a focus on job creation; • create urban planning frameworks to support avoid–shift–improve concept to address transport needs; • shift fuel usage from high to low, or lower carbon sources through decommissioning and or emission ceilings; • remove fossil fuel and power sector subsidies that are not targeted to vulnerable populations; and • create frameworks to encourage private sector investment in the energy sector especially in renewable energy-based power generation and energy efficiency. ⊘ Engage with international best practices and capacity building to support new approaches to energy sector development, considering regional approaches where appropriate. ⊘ Support targeted cross-sector interventions such as health, education, etc. ⊘ Engage evolutions of governance and policy development in energy sector to support improved financial management and private sector involvement. **Energy Utilities** ⊘ Engage in energy sector planning and plan for system development, identifying short-, medium-, and long-term investments to meet clean and low-carbon energy pathway. ⊘ Analyze demand pattern change by COVID-19 and identify critical path in system development including deferral, cancellation, or acceleration of planned projects. Also, consider retirement of inefficient and/or aging assets. ⊘ Deploy grid-strengthening projects to ensure ongoing reliability and remove barriers to enable grid access for renewable power generation. ⊘ Address gender gaps in hiring practices to ensure inclusive staffing. ⊘ Develop flexibility resources in the power sector to improve power system operation and enable larger shares of variable renewable integration: • large-scale energy storage measures for ancillary services and system balancing; and • consider development of demand-side resources in industrial, commercial, and residential sectors including dynamic pricing.

continued on next page

Table 5 continued

Recovery through Rejuvenation and Resilience	Stakeholder Action
	Regulators ➲ Design and strengthen regulatory frameworks to support technical and financial sustainability of utilities (such as full-cost recovery tariffs, reduced cross-subsidization, or non-wire alternatives to system development).[a] ➲ Introduce performance-based regulations for natural monopolies such as transmission and distribution companies. ➲ Introduce energy efficiency standards/labeling for buildings and end-use appliances. ➲ Encourage distributed energy installations (e.g., rooftop solar) and facilitate their grid connection. ➲ Renew focus on priority pollutants with readily quantifiable public health effects (sanitation, hygiene, solid waste disposal, particulate matter, nitrogen oxide, sulfur oxide, etc.). ➲ Enable new and innovative business models to support energy sector development such as increased private sector participation and power purchase agreement transparency.
	End users ➲ Deploy energy-efficient end-use equipment to reduce energy demand including utilities (i.e., water, sewage, telecom), industry and institutional, commercial, and residential buildings. ➲ Engage in end-user programs such as demand response or time of use pricing to support power system optimization. ➲ Deploy distributed renewable energy (e.g., rooftop solar, energy storage behind meters).
	Financiers[b] ➲ Target financing for infrastructure and programs that align with national and international clean and low-carbon energy systems. ➲ Support governments and utilities to develop plans and projects that can be financed. ➲ Use of "shadow" carbon prices to orient investments toward low-carbon solutions and avoid stranded assets.[c]
	Private Sector ➲ Engage in energy planning to provide expert advice on solutions and private sector participation (including job creation) in energy sector development. ➲ Develop solutions to meet current market needs while anticipating future system developments. ➲ Support in-country capacity building for modern energy sector development. ➲ Develop innovative low-carbon technologies with new business models. ➲ Engage with communities to determine needs, hire local staff to support rollout and operations and maintenance of solutions and collection of tariffs.
Improve energy sector resilience and security to a broad range of crises including climate, markets, and pandemics	**DMC Governments** ➲ Engage with stakeholders to identify energy sector resilience and security vulnerabilities to a broad range of crises. ➲ Anticipate subsequent waves of COVID-19 as well as long-term shifts in end-use sector energy demand and plan for effects to energy system operation, maintenance, and development. ➲ Use risk-based planning to address vulnerabilities in the context of overall energy planning. ➲ Consider the opportunities for regional energy trade and integration against national security of supply. ➲ Identify and facilitate opportunities to increase indigenous renewable energy production. ➲ Document recent learnings from COVID-19 resilience and build upon for future responses to crises. ➲ Create programs for capacity building required to mitigate job losses and create new green jobs, such as reskilling, training, job facilitation, and direct public sector employment.

continued on next page

Table 5 continued

Recovery through Rejuvenation and Resilience	Stakeholder Action
	Energy Utilities ◉ Identify utility specific vulnerabilities to crises and develop procedures to address with short-, medium-, and long-term investments. ◉ Build capacity within staff to anticipate and respond to crises. ◉ Include resilience in all parts of planning, operations and maintenance as an ongoing exercise to improve overall system reliability. ◉ Work with end users to determine their energy needs in the context of specific crises and develop support programs (with private sector, where appropriate). ◉ Consider the evolution of local and regional energy sector (i.e., security of operation with high share renewable energy use or increased severe weather conditions due to climate change) in resilience planning.
	Regulators ◉ Encourage and enable energy resilience and security investments by allowing cost recovery to ensure long-term least-cost sector investment pathways.
	Financiers ◉ Include resilience considerations with risk evaluations and project investment decisions. ◉ Provide finances for resilience and energy security investments with support to stakeholders to develop bankable projects.
	End users ◉ Produce an energy needs assessment in the context of a various crises and develop a plan to address vulnerabilities.
	Private Sector ◉ Include resilience considerations in product offerings.[d] ◉ Work with end users to determine sustainable approaches that can offer both climate mitigation and resilience solutions.
Accelerate energy access to poor and vulnerable, particularly for clean cooking	**DMC Governments** ◉ Develop or update targets for energy access for electricity and heating and cooling (including cooking). ◉ Engage with stakeholders, including financiers, and private sector to develop policy and technical solutions and business models. ◉ Provide capital cost support and tariff subsidies where cost recovery is not initially viable. ◉ Measure and monitor progress and evaluate support mechanisms on a regular basis and adjust as needed, with a goal to eliminate any support beyond market measures. ◉ Support end users in the development of productive uses for energy resources, such as through micro and small-scale businesses, schools, and health clinics. ◉ Identify women as one of the vulnerable groups for providing subsidy.
	Energy Utilities ◉ Support targets through deployment of energy access solutions together with private sector. ◉ Develop business models through the piloting and deployment of more distributed power supply, and microgrids and/or minigrids. ◉ Increase focus on other energy access needs such as cooking, heating, and transport.
	Regulators ◉ Develop and encourage pro-poor and pro-vulnerable tariff structures. ◉ Remove regulator barriers to energy access solutions and open up to private sector where needed.
	Financiers ◉ Engage with technology providers and utilities to determine bankable structures for access to energy solutions.

continued on next page

Table 5 continued

Recovery through Rejuvenation and Resilience	Stakeholder Action

Advanced technology and cross-sector interventions including specific technologies	**DMC Governments**
	● Determine country-specific and regional opportunities for advanced technology development, feasibility study, pilot demonstration, and deployment.
	● Create road map with target numbers and milestones, along with supportive policy pathways to mitigate investment risk of private companies.
	● Provide funding and incentives to stakeholders for use of innovative technologies and business models across a broad range of technologies.[e]
	● Engage with the international energy community to create partnerships, build innovation capacity, and learn best-in-class approaches.
	● Develop and deploy programs on end-user energy efficiency, including a focus on heating and cooling systems that can be used to reduce COVID-19 transmission.[f]
	● Identify cross-sector approaches to leverage solutions to address multiple problems such as:
	  • Develop cold chain infrastructure initially to support vaccine delivery, but also in support of the health care sector, in general, as well as other societal needs such as agricultural and fisheries;
	  • Use waste-to-energy to address COVID-19 medical waste (and other waste streams), while addressing power generation gaps for the health care sector and overall power system;
	  • Consider electrification of transport to address urban air pollution, and use of electric vehicles and other modifications to transport infrastructure based on indoor air quality and social distancing requirements;
	  • Deploy rooftop solar PV (together with battery backup when practical) on schools and public infrastructure to help raise awareness and learning on low-carbon innovative technology and for resilient power production;
	  • Support electric vehicle deployments and charging infrastructure;
	  • Develop programs for distributed energy resources such as demand response (including time-of-use rates enabled by smart meters), distributed generation (including co-generation of heat and power), and energy efficiency for urban settings to improve livability of cities.
	
	Energy Utilities
	● Evaluate opportunities to deploy alternative technological solutions to address system issues and address high upfront costs through business models and programmatic approaches.
	● Work with other stakeholders to adjust policy and regulatory changes needed to deploy innovative solutions (such as capacity markets to support power system flexibility). Include capacity building for awareness for end users and other stakeholders not directly engaged in energy system development.
	● Deploy best-in-class and up-to-date solutions when extending or upgrading energy system infrastructure, and measure and evaluation outcome to determine scale-up opportunities.
	● Engage with other sectors to determine mutually beneficial solutions (as highlighted in the DMC governments' section above or heating sector development to utilize most appropriate fuel sources).
	
	Regulators
	● Enable exception-based regulation for piloting of new technologies to reduce barriers for new technologies and cross-sector development (such as waste treatment regulation and power generation in waste-to-energy applications).
	● Set performance-based targets (e.g., carbon dioxide/kilowatt-hour) to allow private sector and utilities to choose the most appropriate technology.

continued on next page

Table 5 continued

Recovery through Rejuvenation and Resilience	Stakeholder Action
	Financiers ◉ Support stakeholders in developing bankable business models to support innovative and cross sector technology interventions. ◉ Highlight international and regional examples of innovative and cross-sector innovations.

COVID-19 = coronavirus disease, DMC = developing member country, PV = photovoltaic.

[a] Non-wire alternatives in power sector development include investments such as battery storage, demand side, and energy efficiency programs that can defer or eliminate needed investments in transmission or distribution grids.

[b] The role of institutional investors, such as insurers and pension funds, are included as financiers and are an important source of private sector funding for "building back better" and cofinancing renewable energy investments. Additionally, the insurance industry is an important actor for building resilience through risk transfer and absorbing technology risk.

[c] ADB uses a shadow unit value of $36.30 per ton of carbon dioxide or its equivalent in 2016 prices for 2016 emissions, to be increased by 2% annually in real terms to allow for the potential of increasing marginal damage of global warming over time. ADB. 2017. *Guidelines For the Economic Analysis of Projects*. Manila.

[d] Resilience opportunities could include higher temperature ratings, increased hardening of structural components to withstand more extreme weather, and design changes to limit risk exposure (such as underground cabling as opposed to overhead approaches).

[e] Advanced technologies can include technologies such as solar and wind power for generation, and also include system technologies such as smart meters, smart appliances, and a broad range of smart grid technologies. Applications for hydrogen, carbon capture utilization, and storage and artificial intelligence are important technologies for deep decarbonization that are only commercially viable in specific applications.

[f] S. Balgeman et al. 2020. *Can HVAC System Help Prevent Transmission of COVID-19?* Mckinsey Advanced Industries Practice. 9 July.

Source: Asian Development Bank.

The floating solar photovoltaic power generation panels at the Da Mi hydropower plant in Binh Thuan, Viet Nam. Innovative technologies can help countries address barriers to deploy sustainable energy technologies (photo by Gerhard Joren/Asian Development Bank).

4 ADB Support to Developing Member Countries in the Energy Sector

Strengths of and Opportunities for the ADB Energy Sector

Cross-Sector Support

Over the past 10 years, from 2011–2020, ADB approved nearly $37.4 billion in energy projects, of which $20.5 billion worth was categorized as clean energy (Figure 6). A large share of projects that were not categorized as clean energy were investments in transmission and distribution infrastructure, which support access to energy, improved grid efficiency, and can strengthen grids to support increasing shares of variable renewable deployments.

Figure 6: Share of Energy Sector Lending, 2011–2020

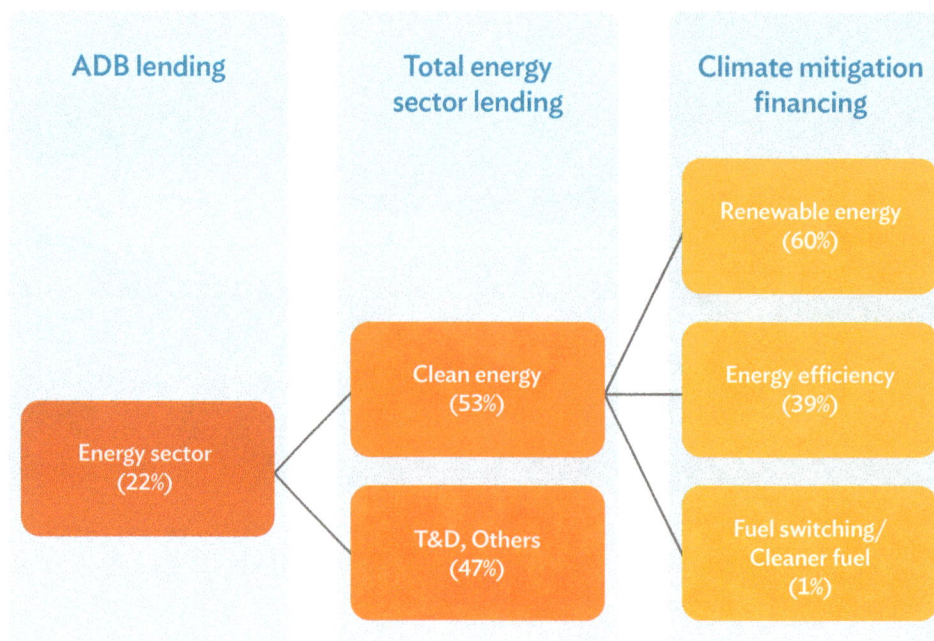

T&D = transmission and distribution.

Source: Asian Development Bank.

ADB's Strategy 2030, approved in 2018, presents a vision for ADB lending organized around seven operational priorities to which energy is an enabling input and plays a role in delivering on each priority (Table 6). Since the energy sector (including the combustion of fossil fuels in the transport sector) makes up approximately two-thirds of global carbon dioxide emissions, these investments play a significant role in addressing climate change mitigation and adaptation.

Table 6: ADB's Energy Project Contributions to Strategy 2030 Operational Priorities in 2020

OP	Strategy 2030 Operational Priority	Number of Projects
OP1	Addressing remaining poverty and reducing inequalities	20
OP2	Accelerating progress in gender equality	28
OP3	Tackling climate change, building disaster resilience	31
OP4	Making cities more livable	7
OP5	Promoting rural development and food security	8
OP6	Strengthening governance and institutional capacity	17
OP7	Fostering regional cooperation and integration	4

OP = operational priority.
Note: Some projects contribute to several OPs in a crosscutting manner.

Source: Asian Development Bank.

ADB Energy Sector during the Response Phase to COVID-19

In 2020, $4.2 billion in loans have been approved in the energy sector by ADB. Due to COVID-19, challenges have been experienced in delivering this program because DMC priorities for allocation of resources have focused on the pandemic and field work has been prevented as a result of both local and international travel restrictions. During the response phase, interventions by ADB's energy sector and private sector operations can be defined as:

(i) knowledge products and strategic studies,

(ii) targeted support to countries and private sector response to the pandemic, and

(iii) delivery of the overall lending pipeline in preparation and support to the recovery phase.

Knowledge products and strategic studies included the development of a technical assistance on virus-resilient and efficient centralized air conditioning in public buildings, and a guidance note on managing infectious medical waste generated during the COVID-19 pandemic. A technical report is also being developed on cold chain technology that can support vaccine delivery in DMCs. South Asia Energy Division initiated a post-COVID-19 urban energy resilience study, integrating inclusive energy infrastructure and health systems. The Pacific Department will conduct analytical economic work on the impact of the pandemic on energy security. This will include a review of the macroeconomic impact of COVID-19 on imported fuel prices, quantities and patterns of electricity demand, trends in fuel imports on the balance of payments of countries, and government fiscal space. These aspects will assist governments to identify and confirm if de-carbonization and improving energy security can be a national imperative that reduces fragility concerns (apart from climate change benefits). Moreover, the Pacific Department has initiated a series of virtual talks with chief executive officers of the Pacific utility companies and with the Pacific Power Association to discuss COVID-19 effects on their operations, post-pandemic planning and challenges, and new post-COVID-19 activities and investment needs.

Private Sector Operations Department led the response to provide liquidity support for several utilities and project developers. A $20 million loan was approved in March 2020 to the PRC—COVID-19 Emergency Energy Supply Project for China Gas to support business continuity in Wuhan City and Hubei Province—as the first country to be faced with managing the pandemic. A $20 million loan was approved in May 2020 to the Electric Networks of Armenia CJSC—COVID-19 Working Capital Support Project to relieve financial stress caused by delayed payments of electricity bills due to COVID-19, which could otherwise lead to deterioration of its services and ultimately disrupt Armenia's access to electricity. A $50 million loan to the ReNew Power COVID-19 Liquidity Support Project in India provides short-term liquidity facility to help tide over the impact of market disruptions due to COVID-19. Several other investments of this nature focused on addressing the very near-term liquidity needs of utilities and project developers.

All energy sector actors at ADB have endeavored to deliver on the originally planned pipeline for 2020. The interventions would help enable reliable and continuous high-quality power supply essential for economic activities in DMCs and for post-pandemic economic recovery, particularly supporting rural agricultural communities who have been seriously affected by COVID-19 lockdowns. Some adjustments to projects have been considered such as allocating savings from existing loans to COVID-19 response. For example, a reassessment of the Power System Developing Plan for Cambodia has revised demand forecasts considering COVID-19 impact to guide investment planning for Electricité du Cambodge. Monitoring of other utility state-owned enterprises for COVID-19 related liquidity issues has also been conducted.

ADB Energy Sector during the Recovery Phase from COVID-19

ADB's existing energy sector investments align well with the needs of DMCs to recover from the effects of the pandemic. From a macro level, the ADB Energy Sector will continue to focus on acute needs as a result of the pandemic, deliver its existing pipeline, and adjust existing projects to address any changes within their respective DMCs. In this context, energy projects will consider the effects of COVID-19 and make adjustments, but there is still a strong and compelling need for energy investments in DMCs that are aligned with the Paris Agreement, UN SDGs, and ADB Strategy 2030. Therefore, no major change in direction and approach is expected, but will seek ways to accelerate clean energy development objectives set even prior to the pandemic.

A key strength of ADB is the presence of staff in over 40 resident missions. While staffing in resident missions has been disrupted by the pandemic, in the near-term existing relationships can be maintained through virtual communications, but as recovery starts to happen, this will allow ADB to rapidly reengage in respective countries. Direct engagement with governments and stakeholders will be essential for developing loans that are best suited for each DMC.

Specifically, ADB's efforts in the recovery phase can be summarized in the following five areas:
    (i)   policy dialogue to support DMC green recovery focusing on renewables and energy efficiency,
    (ii)   transmission and distribution investments to support mitigation and resilience,
    (iii) piloting innovative technologies and ADB processes,
    (iv) development of knowledge products on leading-edge and future technologies, and
    (v)   cross-sector support.

Policy Dialogue to Support Green Recovery in Developing Member Countries

As a long-term partner of Asia and the Pacific DMCs, ADB is well-placed to engage in policy dialogue to support a green recovery from COVID-19. The investments that will be made to support recovery can be used to address targeted and structural issues within the energy sector, as a way to accelerate alignment with UN SDGs and the Paris Agreement. It also ensures that technology is not deployed in the absence of supporting policy, regulation, and governance structures. ADB can provide technical assistance support to determine country-specific priorities, and develop a policy and governance road map on its own or alongside policy or results-based lending modalities to provide the framework and actions to further DMC actions for a green recovery.

For many countries, it has become clear that energy demand will take several years to recover to pre-pandemic levels. Under work-from-home arrangements, energy demand in office and industrial districts has decreased, while energy demand in residential districts has increased. This has resulted in change in load flow mainly in distribution network, as well as changes in daily load curves. To respond these changes, utilities' dispatching operators need to be revised and in the short and medium term, the network expansion plan needs to be adjusted. ADB may support the change in operation and planning since near-term investments may either be delayed or could be reconsidered to take advantage of technology developments, address operation changes, or to address broader shifts in sector development objectives with stronger focus on climate and sustainable development. This provides an opportunity for ADB to engage and support in energy sector development to ensure that investments are, as much as possible, future-proofed and the risk of stranded assets can be mitigated.

The policy dialogue can include increased efforts to mainstream gender and poverty reduction within investments in the energy sector, such as (i) special targets for the electrification of poor households headed by women and socially disadvantaged groups, (ii) improving affordability through targeted subsidy for poor women and vulnerable consumers, (iii) promoting gender-friendly workplace policies in energy utilities that enable more women to work in the sector, and (iv) raising targeted consumer awareness especially for women consumers about the safe and efficient use of energy.

Transmission and Distribution Investments to Support Mitigation and Resilience

Over the last 10 years, approximately 55% of ADB's energy sector investments have been allocated for power sector transmission and distribution. Over that same period, there have been significant development and cost reductions in smart grid technologies[51] as well as renewable energy technologies such as PVs and wind power. Transmission and distribution grids remain an essential backbone of energy sector development, linking supply and demand in a coordinated and reinforcing manner that can support both climate mitigation and resilience. ADB will continue to invest in transmission and distribution, continually evolving to use best-in-class innovative technologies, and look for opportunities to deploy new solutions such as battery storage to better optimize the power grid.

Within this part of ADB investments there is an increased need to address access to energy for which large-scale transmission and distribution networks may not offer the optimal solution. A range of solutions that include solar home systems, clean cooking technologies, and micro and minigrids can be used. These can be deployed along with or in some cases piloted alongside advanced transmission and distribution projects. A good example is in the Meghalaya province in India where ADB is supporting a $166 million project that will not only strengthen and modernize the power distribution network, but also support pilot testing of gender and socially inclusive renewable minigrid energy systems, which have the potential for future replication.[52] This approach builds on the strength of ADB's past investments and extends this to meet the last-mile connection requirements. This could be applied in both rural situations, island communities, and urban slums that are not connected to the grid.

Innovative Technologies and ADB Processes

Innovative energy technologies can often face barriers to deployment in DMCs, including the lack of capacity and experience to implement locally. This applies even when the technology is reasonably mature and already common in other countries. In this context, it is essential to pilot technologies in DMCs to provide support and allow stakeholders to learn and use these technologies within their own countries. For example, pilot floating PV systems will be deployed in Afghanistan, Azerbaijan, and the Kyrgyz Republic as a way to showcase the technology.[53] A number of other technologies are highlighted in Table 5, but this list too is not exhaustive. Additional pilot projects and capacity building within ADB on how to deliver these efficiently will facilitate advances in DMC energy sector development.

ADB is also applying innovative approaches to support technology providers in DMCs. Several competitions have been conducted over the last 2 years, for example, the ADB Energy Sector Technology Innovation Challenge,[54] wherein participants were encouraged to submit proposals under these categories:
 (i) efficient heating and/or cooling solutions,
 (ii) artificial intelligence for energy demand management, and
 (iii) renewable energy-based microgrids.

---

[51] Smart grid technologies include a broad range of utility, network, and end-user technologies that can support the operation grid through ICT. These include smart meters, voltage and frequency monitoring and control, automated protection and recovery equipment, as well as end-user technologies such as building energy management systems, electric vehicle charging, and battery technology.
[52] ADB. 2020. India: Meghalaya Power Distribution Sector Improvement Project.
[53] ADB. 2018. Regional: Floating Solar Energy Development.
[54] The Energy Sector Technology Innovation Challenge was supported by the ADB High-Level Technology Fund. https://challenges.adb.org/en/challenges/technology-innovation-challenge?lang=en.

Over 100 proposals were received, and three winners were chosen on a competitive basis and will each be supported with $500,000 to support their proposal. This unique approach for ADB can support the deployment of innovative technologies in developing countries by the private sector in a way that conventional business processes may not facilitate.

From a process perspective, supporting DMC response and recovery provides an opportunity to identify new ways for ADB to do its work. Adjusting disbursements or processing programs to support emergency liquidity crises, supporting health care sector efforts by adjusting implementation or processing new programs to support cold chain needs for vaccine distribution, increasing livelihood components of programs to better support economic recovery, and evaluating flexible contracting options are just a few examples of ways that ADB can respond. The urgent need to support DMCs has challenged ADB management to test new approaches and encourage innovation in its processes.

Knowledge Products on Leading-Edge and Future Technologies

It is important to support DMCs with information that can be used to determine appropriate technologies for energy sector development. The barriers and enablers to technology deployment have to be systematically identified, assessed, and then addressed to facilitate the adoption and integration of future technologies by DMCs. Knowledge products on leading-edge and future technologies must then be disseminated to appropriate DMC stakeholders so that knowledge and innovation can be utilized to scale up technology adoption and address barriers that include policy, regulation, financing, and governance. Consideration of a holistic context ensures that technologies can be suitably integrated in existing systems, or changes are facilitated to accommodate scaled-up deployment.

The aspects listed above are considered both in pilot projects supported by ADB and in knowledge products developed. ADB has developed handbooks on technologies that are projected to benefit many countries, including:

   (i)   battery energy storage system,[55]
   (ii) microgrids for power quality and connectivity, [56]
   (iii) waste to energy,[57] and
   (iv) hydrogen (under development).

Ongoing technical assistance support is also helping countries develop plans for energy sector development. For example, as part of the subproject Energy System Analysis, Technology Road Maps, and Feasibility Studies for Pilot Testing, under the cluster technical assistance on Integrated High Impact Innovation in Sustainable Energy Technology, work is ongoing to develop regional and several country baseline energy outlooks until 2040 as basis for projecting low-carbon and decarbonization scenarios.

As each country and region will have unique circumstances and priorities that need to be addressed during the recovery period, ADB initiatives will need to be both targeted and responsive. Much of the ongoing planning that has been set out will remain relevant, but adjustments will also be required as new needs arise. Examples could include:

---

[55] ADB. 2018. *Handbook on Battery Energy Storage System*. Manila.
[56] ADB. 2020. *Handbook on Microgrids for Power Quality and Connectivity*. Manila.
[57] ADB. 2020. *Waste to Energy in the Age of Circular Economy: Best Practice Handbook*. Manila.

Support DMCs to prepare safety nets for some utility customers who cannot pay due to job loss. Knowledge sharing of financing schemes applied in other countries could be beneficial.

Provide DMCs with knowledge products to support utility O&M labor force as essential workers, offering guidance on best practices to ensure they are protected from COVID-19 infection. For example, some utilities in advanced countries and in project developments have started activities like drone inspection of overhead power transmission lines instead of traditional visual inspection by O&M staff.

Support power utilities to accelerate O&M automation and/or remote control of grid facilities by financing relevant projects, e.g., smart grid, digital technology, and SCADA/EMS.[58]

Cross-Sector Support

The provision of energy is essential for the delivery of virtually all aspects of development. As highlighted earlier, energy is needed to provide core urban services. Energy is needed to deliver health care in rural clinics and schools, often through solar power systems. In agriculture, particularly for DMCs, solar water pumps provide an efficient and cost-effective approach to delivering irrigation. Electric vehicles need reliable power systems to supply their batteries. Information and communication technologies in schools used for teaching and learning can be powered by renewable energy.

In the COVID-19 recovery phase, vaccines will be available to prevent the spread of the disease and widespread vaccine delivery will be required in rural and urban areas. ADB will consider the use of renewable energy for rural health centers and maintain a cold chain for vaccines, as well as ways to support urban cold chains through efficient technology and work with the transport sector on efficient mobile refrigerated vehicles. While this will entail cost in the short term, in the long term this can provide better energy service and enabling infrastructure to the health sector, and also help other sectors.

These examples highlight the opportunity for ADB's energy sector initiatives to engage across all development sectors to support the needs of DMCs in order to meet their development objectives. Cross-sector collaboration will provide ADB the opportunity to address development issues and deliver services in a truly sustainable manner in DMCs.

---

[58] SCADA/EMS stands for Supervisory Control and Data Acquisition and Energy Management System.

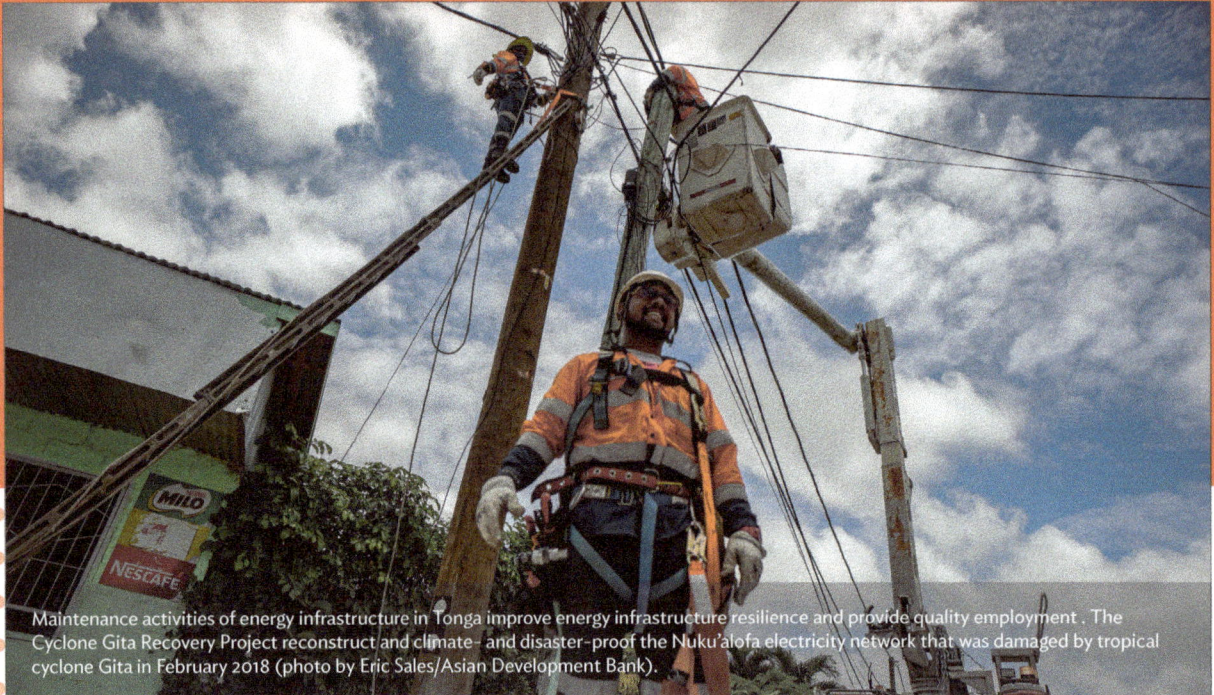

Maintenance activities of energy infrastructure in Tonga improve energy infrastructure resilience and provide quality employment . The Cyclone Gita Recovery Project reconstruct and climate- and disaster-proof the Nuku'alofa electricity network that was damaged by tropical cyclone Gita in February 2018 (photo by Eric Sales/Asian Development Bank).

5 Conclusion

COVID-19 has disrupted the global economy. The energy sector has responded to continue and maintain power supply to support other sectors, but has also been affected in ways that may profoundly change the future of its development. ADB and a broad group of energy sector stakeholders will continue to deliver the vision to develop a sustainable energy system for all. The COVID-19 pandemic has provided a great challenge and opportunity to address gaps within the energy sector especially around climate change mitigation and resilience. The adoption of clean energy technologies will help the sector recover from the pandemic can make sustainable energy for all a reality.

This guidance note has provided a range of actions and solutions that can be adopted and implemented by stakeholders in ADB DMCs and by ADB itself in response and recovery phases to COVID-19. It is clear that not all these actions will be appropriate for every country and that a context-specific evaluation of needs and opportunities must be carried out in difrerent countries and regions. This aligns with the country-focused approach highlighted in ADB's Strategy 2030.

COVID-19 has provided the motivation to find solutions that can meet both short- and long-term energy sector needs, and stakeholders must work together in order to ensure that projects support broader societal recovery from the pandemic. As highlighted in the introduction, the next step following this report is to develop country-specific recovery plans using the following four pillars:

(i)   enhancing sustainable energy services;
(ii) improving energy sector resilience and security;
(iii) accelerating energy access to the poor and vulnerable, particularly for clean cooking; and
(iv) applying advanced technology and cross-sector interventions.

Using these principles along with strengths of its development work in Asia and the Pacific, ADB's energy sector programs will be at the forefront of these efforts, and will continue to increase its engagement across all development needs and deliver energy services in a truly sustainable manner.